FINDING THEIR OWN PLACE

FINDING THEIR OWN PLACE:

YOUTH IN THREE SMALL RURAL COMMUNITIES TAKE PART IN INSTRUCTIVE SCHOOL-TO-WORK EXPERIENCES

by
Bruce A. Miller
and
Karen J. Hahn

Clearinghouse on Rural Education and Small Schools
Charleston, West Virginia

ERIC°

Clearinghouse on Rural Education and Small Schools
Appalachia Educational Laboratory
PO Box 1348, Charleston, WV 25325

Cover illustration by John MacDonald, Williamstown, MA
Cover design by Richard Hendel, Chapel Hill, NC

Library of Congress Cataloging-in-Publication Data

Miller, Bruce A.
  Finding their own place: youth in three small rural communities take part in instructive school-to-work experiences / by Bruce A. Miller and Karen J. Hahn.
    p. cm.
  Includes bibliographical references (p.) and index.
  ISBN 1-880785-18-8
  1. Education, Cooperative—United States—Case studies. 2. School-to-work transition—United States—Case studies. 3. United States—Rural conditions—Case studies. 4. Community development—United States—Case studies. 5. Community and school—United States—Case studies.
  I. Hahn, Karen J., 1970- . II. Title.
  LC1049.5.M55 1997
  371.2'27—dc21   97-30278
                                                             CIP

This publication was prepared with funding from the U.S. Department of Education, Office of Educational Research and Improvement, under contract no. RR93002012. The opinions expressed herein do not necessarily reflect the positions or policies of the Appalachia Educational Laboratory, the Office of Educational Research and Improvement, or the Department of Education.

The ERIC Clearinghouse on Rural Education and Small Schools is operated by the Appalachia Educational Laboratory (AEL), Inc. AEL is an Affirmative Action/Equal Opportunity Employer.

Table of Contents

Preface viii
Rural Communities Face Unique Challenges ix

Chapter 1. Review of the Research on School-to-Work 1
The Need to Refocus Educational Practices 1
    Two-Tiered Educational System 3
School-to-Work Initiative 4
School-to-Work Transition in Rural Communities 6
    Challenges to Rural Communities 6
The Secretary's Commission on Achieving Necessary
    Skills (SCANS) 9

Portraits of Three Rural Communities 11
Introduction to Chapters 2, 3, and 4 11

Chapter 2. Broadus, Montana: Involving Youth in
    Community Development 13
Goals 13
    The Community Development Project 14
    Broadus's Progress in Community-School Partnering 16
Student Involvement and Workplace Competencies 18
    Community/School Development Partnership 20
    Task Force Committee Activity 21
    Broadus County High School Community Development Course 23
    Cross-Grade Tutoring 26
Conclusion 28

Chapter 3. Saco, Montana: Creating the Extraordinary
    with Kids 33
Goals 33
    Using Technology to Enhance Learning Opportunities 34
    Using Extracurricular Activities to Extend Learning 40
    Making Learning Relevant to Students' Needs 42
Conclusion 50

Chapter 4. Methow Valley, Washington: Community
  as Classroom 53
Goals 53
Origin and Focus of School-to-Work Programming 54
  Program Components 56
  Getting the Word Out 65
Conclusion 69

Chapter 5. Policy Implications for Planning and Development
  in Rural Settings 71
Rethinking the Role of the School 71
Three Approaches to Building Community-School Linkages 72
Strategies for Change 74
The Importance of Policy in Creating and Sustaining............................ 77
  Community-School Linkages.. 77
  Strategies for Developing Effective Policy Support 78
Conclusion 81

Appendices
  A   Using SCANS as an Interpretive Framework 83
  B   Powder River Region Community Development Goals 88
  C   Methow Valley as a Classroom: Sample Forms 89
  D   Resource Documents 96

References 101

Index 105

About the Authors 113

List of Tables

Table 1. SCANS Competency and Foundation Areas 10

Table 2. Context of the Three Schools:
Demographic Characteristics 11

Table 3. CDP Progress Chart for Broadus, Montana 17

Table 4. Sources of Funding for Innovation at the
Saco School District 38

Table 5. Percentage of Students Who Participate in
School Organizations 42

Table 6. The Sequence of Events, Adult Support, and Student
Learning in the Development of a Youth Recreation Center 44

Table 7. Dimensions of the Ideal Learning Environment 51

Table 8. Methow Valley as a Classroom—Selected Offerings 57

Table 9. The Ten Most Frequently Mentioned Attributes Leading
to Successful Community-Based Learning for Students 75

Table 10. The Relationship Between SCANS Competencies
and Broadus Activities 85

Table 11. The Relationship Between SCANS Competencies
and Selected Saco Activities 86

Table 12. The Relationship Between SCANS Competencies
and Methow Valley Activities 87

List of Figures

Figure 1. A Comparison of Three U.S. Workforce
Production Sectors 3

Figure 2. Short-Term Action Planning Form 25

Preface

This publication documents educational practices that hold promise for rural communities struggling to survive in economically and socially difficult times. Research and development work is under way in many rural areas in the United States to help communities address the challenges they face (Nachtigal, Haas, Parker, & Brown, 1989; Delargy, Hubel, Luther, & Wall, 1992; Miller, 1993a). One promising line of research and development focuses on ways rural schools can serve the social, economic, and environmental well-being of their communities. This research sheds light on ways schools can benefit from closer ties to the community by providing opportunities for community-based learning through community service and career exploration. On the other hand, community groups and organizations with development goals can benefit from collaborations with schools by involving students in conducting surveys, gathering data through interviews, or directly serving on a local task force. Such opportunities help youth develop the skills useful in today's ever-changing workplace.

The Education and Work and the Rural Education programs at Northwest Regional Educational Laboratory collaborated on the development of this resource monograph for use in rural communities, especially those that are remote and small. This monograph might help school personnel and community members think about new ways of collaborating.

- Educators will learn about promising practices for school-to-work programs and how schools and communities can work together to better meet the needs of youth. They will also discover strategies for linking and integrating community-based learning opportunities with academic subjects.
- Administrators will learn the importance of building a strong support base for bringing about school reform. They will also find successful strategies for sustaining the changes over time.
- Community development practitioners will learn to see the school as an important player in addressing community needs.
- Community members—parents, students, and other residents—will gain a greater appreciation and understanding of what it means to live in a rural setting. They will learn how academic goals can be achieved through community-based learning experiences and expanded through distance technology.

This report is divided into three sections:
- Chapter 1 briefly reviews the research on school-to-work issues, focusing on how the unique qualities of rural communities create special

challenges for the development and implementation of school-to-work programs.
- Chapters 2 through 4 present portraits of three rural schools that have worked closely with their communities to engage youth in experiences that benefit their communities and prepare youth to be productive members of a democratic society. The conclusion of each portrait includes a discussion of how lessons learned in these communities can be applied in other locations.
- Chapter 5 addresses the importance of policy development as a tool for garnering support for school-to-work program development and for helping sustain innovative changes.

Rural Communities Face Unique Challenges

Rural schools and communities face unique problems that differentiate them from their metropolitan counterparts. For example, rural communities tend to be geographically isolated, have low population density, and suffer from economic and population decline. They also may lack local services. For example, many rural communities have a single grocery store, minimal social services, no factories, no radio station or movie theater, and no dentist. These conditions often limit student exposure to a variety of workplace opportunities and experiences. By comparison, metropolitan areas possess a wealth of diverse workplace settings that can provide opportunities for students to learn and to experience the world of work. Without these work-related resources, rural communities and their schools must use creative approaches for helping youth obtain the competencies for a successful school-to-work transition. The need for innovation applies whether high school graduates pursue further education or immediately seek work in the city or in their own communities.

In addition, the world economic situation has created a climate demanding self-assessment and reform regarding the role and purpose of education in preparing youth for the future. Traditional basic skills education may not be an adequate approach to helping young people secure meaningful work in a rural environment. While fewer than 25 percent of today's jobs require a college degree, forecasters predict that 70 percent of the jobs in the next decade will require some form of postsecondary training (Harrington-Lueker, 1993). Low skill, high-wage jobs are drying up in rural settings. Previous opportunities for resource-based employment and low-level manufacturing have all but disappeared in many parts of the country. Currently, rural America suffers from the highest unemployment rates in the United States, a rate of poverty that is growing twice as fast as that found in metropolitan areas, a 10 percent decrease in median family income, and a wide-scale exodus of the young and educated seeking employment in metropolitan centers. These changes have seen the decline of too many once-viable rural communities.

Given these changes, the time has come for innovative approaches to preparing young people for the world of work and to finding and creating value in our rural communities. This report demonstrates three interpretations of school-to-work programming as a means of investing in both young people and the rural communities they live in.

CHAPTER 1

Review of the Research on School-to-Work

The Need to Refocus Educational Practices

The School-to-Work Opportunities Act was passed into law in 1994 (Boland, 1995). Congress authorized funds for fiscal year 1994 and again for 1995 to help communities mold apprenticeships, tech-prep programs, vocational education, cooperative education, service learning strategies, and other potential resources into comprehensive school-to-work transition programs (Northwest Regional Educational Laboratory [NWREL], 1994). The aim is to provide career counseling and labor force knowledge and skills for all students to better prepare them for today's global marketplace.

The need for school-to-work programs has grown from a recognition that most of our nation's schools focus on and direct their resources toward preparing students for college (Government Accounting Office [GAO], 1993) while failing to address the needs of a great many noncollege-bound youth. Many schools tend to measure their success by the percentage of students who go to college (Washington Governor's Council, 1995). High school counselors also tend to advise students about colleges, not careers (Kazis, 1993). These trends expose the underlying view in this country that a college degree is the best route to occupational advancement and careers. This college focus warrants concern because the majority of young people do not graduate from postsecondary education programs.

Nationally, 50 percent of high school seniors enter some form of postsecondary program after they graduate from high school. Of these, half (equaling about 25 percent) successfully complete a baccalaureate program sometime within their lifetime (Kazis, 1993). Research from the Government Accounting Office (1991) shows only 15 percent of incoming college freshmen go on to earn a degree from a four-year college within six years of high school graduation. Many of the remaining 85 percent of these young people spend the six years following their high school graduation drifting between educational and occupational experiences. For the most part, they do not gain skills or knowledge appropriate for today's workplace. These statistics raise serious concern among educators and the general public about what our schools are doing to prepare youth for postsecondary experiences.

On the status of these young people finding jobs, Richard Kazis (1993) comments:

> These young Americans are generally ill-prepared while in school for the world of work they are about to enter. They receive little guidance on how to move into a career that can support a family. Their reading, writing, math, and communications skills are generally inadequate for the demands of today's quality employers. They are shut out from jobs in many of the nation's most stable, high-paying, and high-status large employers. (p. 1)

There are serious consequences of this ill-preparedness for these individuals, as well as for our country's economy. Many of these unskilled workers will find themselves in minimum wage jobs that have high rates of turnover; lack career ladders; and have minimal, if any, fringe benefits. Furthermore, high school graduates who do not go on to postsecondary programs are having greater difficulty in sustaining economic independence relative to their better-educated peers (Baron, 1994). Business owners and leaders are also affected. Employers claim to have difficulty finding employees with the academic, analytical, and technical skills they need (NWREL, 1994).

Many different forces contribute to the skill shortage. Education is a crucial player since one of its roles is to prepare youth to be competent and productive citizens and workers. In our efforts to reform our educational institutions, changes in the economy must be considered. Since the mechanization of agriculture, mining, and other industries, we have seen the steady decline of job opportunities in various sorts of rural production. Currently, U.S. de-industrialization has resulted in the loss of many well-paying blue-collar jobs as they are exported to other countries or replaced through technological advances.

Employment opportunities in both agriculture and manufacturing have declined rapidly over the past 20 years (Figure 1). Most of the individuals who occupied these positions lack the skills necessary for transitioning to an economy dominated by the service sector. Moreover, the public school system is not prepared to provide the skills youth need to succeed in the median and upper levels of the service economy.

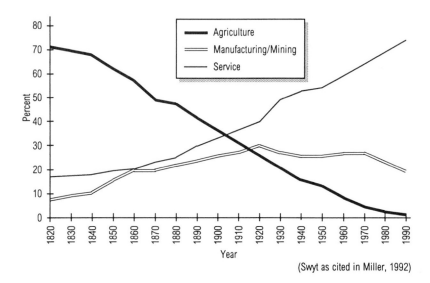

(Swyt as cited in Miller, 1992)

Figure 1. A Comparison of Three U.S. Workforce Production Sectors

Two-Tiered Educational System

Our public education system is essentially a two-tiered system: one tier focuses on college preparation and the other on vocational education. Neither avenue adequately prepares youth for life after high school. The fact that within six years of high school graduation only a small percentage of students complete college substantiates weaknesses in the college preparation tier. Vocational education programs, the other alternative, have been regarded as the track for students who are not headed for college. Unfortunately, fewer resources and less direction have been allocated for vocational pathways (Washington Governor's Council, 1995; Kazis, 1993; O'Neil, 1995). According to Kazis,

The division [between vocational courses and academic courses] perpetuated an unfair tracking system; it failed to provide students with the basic skills they needed to function in the workplace; and it flew in the face of cognitive research on how people learn. (1993, p. 7)

Moreover, neither the academic nor the vocational students receive many marketable skills. Willard Daggett, director of the International Center for Leadership in Education, characterizes the situation:

The [vocational students] don't get the rigor in science and language arts content that is extremely important. The college prep students don't have the ability to apply what theoretical curriculum they have. Schools have not addressed application. And the students in the general track have neither the relevance nor the rigor, so they're in the worst position of all (cited in O'Neil, 1995, p. 47).

Rural schools. Rural communities are affected greatly when schools do not sufficiently prepare their youth for life after high school. The downturn of the 1980s hit rural communities especially hard, and made lasting changes to their economies. As mills, mines, farms, and factories become more mechanized or shut down, young people migrate to urban areas because it has become increasingly difficult to live in rural areas.

Most students do not benefit from the two-tiered academic-vocational education system. When rural schools place the same emphasis as metropolitan schools on college preparation, they tend to lose a steady flow of their youth to the metropolitan areas. Ironically, programs designed to address noncollege-bound youth tend to be hopelessly out of phase with the changing world of work. Rural students are left in "an occupational and educational world about which they have little knowledge and over which they have little control" (DeYoung & Lawrence, 1995, p. 109). The results are devastating to rural communities: Students who go on to postsecondary schools tend to move to metropolitan areas where high-paying, skilled jobs are available.

School-to-Work Initiative

Americans have embarked on a rigorous educational reform agenda. A major piece of this agenda has been an emphasis on better preparing students for life after high school. The narrow focus on college preparation and existing vocational educational programs have come under critical review.

The primary objective of school-to-work programs is to create an education system in which all young people have access to career education and guidance and labor-market information. This includes emphasis on "active, contextual learning, broad rather than narrow skill training, and the integration of academic and vocational education" (Kazis, 1993).

Literature on the school-to-work transition emphasizes the importance of students gaining real-world, hands-on work experience. Students should experience the skills, tools, tasks, time lines, and pressures involved in job situations (Boland, 1995). This involves a comprehensive interactive curriculum, not merely visiting a business site or hearing a guest lecturer once or twice.

The U.S. Department of Labor (DOL) and U.S. Department of Education (DOE), together with leading education and business organizations, have identified three basic components that school-to-work transition programs should encompass in order to be effective (Boland, 1995):

- work-based learning that provides a planned program of job training or experiences, paid work experience, workplace mentoring, and instruction in general workplace competencies and a range of industry-specific elements;

- school-based learning that provides career exploration and counseling, instruction in a career major, a program of study based on high academic and skill standards, at least one year of postsecondary education, and periodic evaluations of students' academic strengths and weaknesses; and

- connecting activities that coordinate the involvement of employers, schools, and students; match students with work-based learning opportunities; and train teachers, mentors, and counselors (p.2).

There is widespread agreement at this point that students need career education and development in order to better prepare them for life after high school, and that the wall separating vocational and academic education needs to be torn down. Students need experiences outside the classroom through internships, cooperative education programs, and youth apprenticeships (GAO, 1993).

Forging links with businesses may be important for schools, but there are other opportunities for students to achieve "real-world" experiences. Rural communities, in particular, will need to look for alternative experiences for students. A combination of time-tested and new ideas may be the best approach, including youth leadership

organizations (Future Farmers of America [FFA], 4-H), providing opportunities to start student-operated businesses, and organizing community service projects. There is no recipe for providing the technical
skills to students that will allow them to go directly into today's labor
force. Instead, the emphasis must be on *learning to learn.*

Early leaders in school-to-work. Florida, Oregon, Tennessee,
and Wisconsin were among the first states to enact statutory provisions
for school-to-work initiatives (GAO, 1993). Washington was recognized nationally as the first to pass legislation to specifically invest state
funds in the development of school-to-work transition programs (Washington Governor's Council, 1995).

School-to-Work Transition in Rural Communities

Rural schools tend to be small, and many are so small that
educational approaches used in metropolitan areas do not work well
(Nachtigal, 1995). Thus, much of the literature on school-to-work,
which lacks a rural focus, is not very useful. This is obvious from the
tremendous emphasis placed on linking schools with local businesses
to provide students with opportunities for practical work experience.
For example, the Governor's Council for the State of Washington's
School-to-Work Transition suggests, "At the local level, intermediary
organizations will convene business, labor, community, and education
leaders, so that all of their combined resources can be marshaled to
help students learn" (1995, p. 18). In an urban area, this is a useful
suggestion. However, how do you follow this when your community is
small and isolated, and when you have few businesses and limited
services?

Challenges to Rural Communities
School-to-work programs are likely to look a little different in
every rural community. They will reflect the unique characteristics and
creativity of each community, drawing upon its available resources,
which may be limited. Although there is great diversity among rural
communities, there are certain similarities that need to be understood
in order for school-to-work to be successful. For instance, people in
rural areas generally live widely dispersed; their communities often are
geographically isolated; resources tend to be limited; and, for many,
economic distress is threatening the community's very livelihood and
existence.

Economic distress. The declining rural economy and mechanization of mining and agriculture has led to high levels of unemployment in many rural communities. Overall, unemployment is higher in rural areas than metropolitan areas. Unemployed rural workers tend to be unemployed 50 percent longer than urban workers, and when they do return to work, they have a much greater chance of accepting a cut in pay (DeYoung & Lawrence, 1995; Sherman, 1992). Moreover, research indicates that rural pay is lower in every field, and that the gap in pay is widening between rural and metro areas (Sherman, 1992). Without a doubt, high unemployment leads to a rural rate of poverty–50 percent higher–than in metropolitan areas (DeYoung, 1995).

Rural students also attend more poorly funded schools. Rural schools, on the average, face higher costs and have lower revenues (Stern, 1994; Sherman, 1992), partly because they serve a small population spread over a wide area. Also, rural communities often find themselves with a low tax base, especially in resource-dependent communities where previously stable industries such as logging, agriculture, and mining have either depleted local resources and shut down or drastically reduced their labor force due to mechanization (Miller, 1990).

Ambivalence toward education. Economic circumstances can breed pessimism and fatalistic attitudes. Some rural people believe their communities do not offer many opportunities for their children. Further, they often do not view the school system as a resource for economic improvement. Alan DeYoung and Barbara Kent Lawrence (1995) saw rural parents vote down local tax increases for education, apparently because the parents rarely saw the utility of such schooling in their own occupational histories. Students sometimes adopt these attitudes as well. Other researchers have discussed how social and geographical marginality have helped prevent youth from buying into the "middle-class folk theory," which promises well-paying jobs to those who achieve well academically and obtain school credentials (Brandau & Collins, 1992, p. 4). Similar sentiments were found by Seal and Harmon (1995) in a community whose livelihood was threatened by the closing of factories:

> The area's blue-collar workers typically associate careers with college-educated, managerial workers–the same people perceived to be the anti-union folks who are responsible for the trend in which well-paying jobs with benefits have been replaced by much lower-paying service jobs with few or no benefits. (p. 123)

Fear of uprooting the community. Another challenge that further fosters this ambivalence is the threat of losing their sense of roots. Community, place, and family often are strong values in rural areas. However, changes in society threaten these values and family life in general. Education contributes to the threat because many of today's educational values run counter to local community values (DeYoung & Lawrence, 1995). Parents perceive that higher education for their children increases the likelihood that they will move away from home and fracture the sense of family unity. Brandau and Collins (1992) summarize the challenges facing rural families:

> The whole notion of education leading to better jobs rests on a middle class assumption of what "better" jobs might be. This assumption is not always shared by poor, rural, working-class people who know that mainstream, professional jobs require moving away, often to a metropolitan area. Given their valuing and experience of physical, outdoor work, there is an ambivalence toward intellectual or office work, which is often seen as less than respectable, and which typically entails social and geographic uprooting. (1992, p. 16)

Under these circumstances, the prospects for implementing any educational reform look slim to nonexistent. However, some rural communities turned the seemingly impossible into success stories for youth and their communities. They have capitalized on their local strengths—small size, sense of community, pride of place—and have fashioned school-to-work opportunities that fit in the unique rural context.

Many rural residents value the isolation, privacy, environment, family-friendly feeling, schools, and sense of roots that small towns provide. These values can unite a community and become a solid basis for building successful school-to-work programs. For example, rural schools frequently possess similar strengths, such as close ties to their community; supportive and inclusive environments; flexibility; and a high degree of student, parent, and community support and participation (Haas & Lambert, 1995). These are excellent traits to draw upon for implementing school-to-work programs. They also resemble the characteristics valued by employers in today's workplace—the ability to work in teams, communicate effectively, solve problems, and learn how to learn (Lewis, 1995).

Rural schools need to explore all possibilities for school-to-work experiences, among them extracurricular clubs and organizations;

service learning; and teaching others about hobbies, talents, or computer skills. The school-to-work focus found in three communities chronicled in the next chapters entails thinking differently about what schools have been doing all along. For example, students in many schools work in offices answering telephones and doing other office tasks. This is real-world experience, which can be documented and included in student portfolios as work experience.

Diana Walters (cited in Alger, 1994) offers several ideas for identifying school-to-work opportunities. For example, many rural towns have a local economic development commission with opportunities to gain real-world experiences. Walters suggests creating opportunities for work-based learning assignments that occur over the summer, encouraging employers to share costs and expand training options, developing service learning projects that require students to interact with the community, and developing school-based enterprise projects using local employers as consultants and mentors (p. 6).

Chapters 2 through 4 present three case study portraits of rural school-to-work projects. The portraits support Walters' belief that opportunities currently exist in most communities or can be created. In fact, given the isolation of many rural communities, they would be far better off building on existing community resources than trying to emulate metropolitan examples. To help rural educators see how local community resources can be used, the Secretary's Commission on Achieving Necessary Skills (SCANS) has been included as a way to view and assess school-to-work opportunities.

The Secretary's Commission on Achieving Necessary Skills

In 1990, the Secretary's Commission on Achieving Necessary Skills (SCANS) defined a common core of skills that constitute job readiness and designed strategies for implementing these skills into school curricula. The commission urged educators to prepare students in two general areas of learning: competencies and a primary foundation. Table 1 provides an overview of these two learning areas.

The first area, competency, reflects workplace skills such as the ability to manage resources, to work amicably and productively with others, to acquire and use information, to master complex systems, and to work with a variety of technologies. The second area, foundation, includes basic literacy and computational skills, the thinking skills necessary to put knowledge to work, and the personal qualities that make workers dedicated and trustworthy.

Table 1. SCANS Competency and Foundation Areas

Competency Area	Foundation Area
Resources—allocating time, money, materials, space, and staff	Basic skills—reading, writing, arithmetic and mathematics, speaking, and listening
Interpersonal skills—working on teams, teaching others, servicing customers, leading, negotiating, and working well with people from culturally diverse backgrounds	Thinking skills—thinking creatively, making decisions, solving problems, seeing things in the mind's eye, knowing how to learn, and reasoning
Information—acquiring and evaluating data, organizing and maintaining files, interpreting and communicating, and using computers to process information	Personal qualities—individual responsibility, self-esteem, sociability, integrity, and self-management
Systems—understanding social, organizational, and technological systems; monitoring and correcting performance; and designing or improving systems	
Technology—selecting equipment and tools, applying technology to specific tasks, and maintaining and troubleshooting technologies	

Two major assumptions about learning underlie the SCANS report. First, learning should be contextualized and, second, students should become actively engaged in their own learning. The commission suggests making students more responsible for their own learning through working with teachers to solve problems.

Implementing the SCANS skills into curricula does not require great changes. The commission suggests that some schools may design new coursework, but this is not necessary. SCANS skills can be integrated into each subject in the core curriculum. Much of what it entails is rethinking how existing subjects are taught. Rather than having students learn in the abstract what they later will need to apply, learning objectives should be provided within real environments–and what better place than the community context. (See Appendix A for more information on SCANS and how it might be used to develop an understanding about school-to-work opportunities in rural communities.)

PORTRAITS OF THREE RURAL COMMUNITIES

Introduction to Chapters 2, 3, and 4

Many rural schools across the country are implementing innovative and beneficial school-to-work programs. The schools featured in the next three chapters provide insights into the sorts of possibilities that existed in their isolated communities, located in the Northwest. Table 2 provides a comparative demographic overview of the three school districts. These school districts were studied because of their reputations for using local community resources in creative and effective ways. Each of the school districts took different routes to addressing the needs of youth for experience-based education.

Table 2. Context of the Three Schools: Demographic Characteristics

School District Name	Size and Organization	Community	Size of Town	Isolation
Broadus County High School	N=180 grades 7-12	Broadus, Montana	<550	78 miles from nearest town of 2,500 or more
Saco School District	N=74 grades 7-12	Saco, Montana	<250	28 miles from nearest town of 2,500 or more
Methow Valley School District	N=378 grades 7-12	Winthrop and Twisp, Washington	<1,000	120 miles from a town of 2,500 or more

CHAPTER 2.

Broadus, Montana: Involving Youth in Community Development

Goals

1. Develop workplace skills and competencies through active participation in community development.
2. Develop leadership through real-world opportunities.
3. Help students appreciate and value their community through active participation in community-based learning.

Broadus, the county seat for Powder River County, Montana, is a small town located on U.S. Highway 212, which connects southeast Montana with South Dakota. Rolling prairie, cattle, sagebrush, and antelope are common sights as you drive through the area into town. Large freight trucks drone on, day and night, as they haul their payloads to destinations far beyond Broadus. Gillette, Wyoming, population 23,200, is 86 miles to the south. Miles City, Montana, population 9,602, is 78 miles to the east. Billings, the largest town in Montana, population 80,500, is a three-hour drive from Broadus, barring bad weather conditions. Isolation poses challenges for the citizens of Broadus, but it also contributes to a valued way of life.

The county high school is situated on the same campus as the elementary school in Broadus. The buildings are relatively up-to-date due to oil revenues generated during the early 1970s, which helped build additions. Most people work in government, education, ranching, farming, and small service businesses, but in recent years other residents have found work in small plane chartering, hunting guide services, and the development of a wagon train tourist event. The county government and the school system employ the largest number of people in the county, and teachers are among the highest-paid people in the county. Student population has declined steadily since the 1980s, though. In 1985, the high school enrollment peaked at 171; by 1993, enrollment had dropped to 127–a 26 percent decline.

Residents of Powder River County made plans to address the declining economic base of their community in the 1970s, but took little action at that time. The school, teachers, and students did not figure into those early plans. Then, in the 1980s, the community experienced an economic upswing due to national demand for local oil reserves. However, by the 1990s, the community once again faced a serious downturn because of declining oil prices and a general decline in extractive industries such as mining and logging.

The downturn threatened the economic viability of Broadus, the county seat. Stores and small shops closed. Medical and social services and employment opportunities rapidly disappeared. At about this time, local leaders became involved in a community and school partnership project sponsored by the Northwest Regional Educational Laboratory.

The Community Development Project

The Rural Education Program at the Northwest Regional Educational Laboratory began pilot testing a model of community development in 1993. The project was designed to enhance the local capacity of small, isolated, and economically distressed rural communities to sustain their social and economic viability through community development activities, using the local school district as a primary resource. The approach, Community/School Development Partnership (CDP), developed around three general goals:

1. Create a structure that empowers the community and the local school district to address community development issues.
2. Develop the knowledge and skills important for community renewal.
3. Implement a plan that engages the community and the school district in a partnership to achieve community-defined development goals.

Students can pursue each goal by working with the adults in their communities. In fact, it became critically important that students, especially in the high school, be engaged in substantive ways.

In rural settings such as Broadus, students represent a continuity with the historical past of their communities and a transition to its future survival. Nine key assumptions underlying the CDP approach help clarify these points:

- Leadership is a skill that is developed through knowledge and practice.
- Ongoing leadership is essential, and current leaders must ensure that new leaders are constantly being trained.
- Community leadership needs to be replenished and reenergized.
- Positive change in a community happens in a planned fashion.
- Preventing problems is more cost effective than trying to correct problems once they occur.
- Rural leaders and communities can learn from the successes of others.
- In small rural communities, the school has the potential to provide facilities, professional staff, energetic students, and a host of re-sources to support community renewal.
- When the school forms a partnership with the community to facili-tate achieving community goals, both the school and the commu-nity are strengthened.
- Once involved, students are a valuable resource in community development, and they develop a new appreciation of their rural community.

Leadership plays a central role in community development. Leaders evolve through training, practice, and exposure to successful leadership models. Therefore, it becomes critically important that leadership be redefined as a shared responsibility rather than a divine right held by few elected or hired individuals. In CDP, leadership skills are taught to a broad range of community members, including stu-dents, and then applied to real-life situations that address community-identified needs. In Broadus, students demonstrated remarkable re-sponsibility, insightfulness, and leadership. However, they are often overlooked in community development planning. In rural communi-ties, where the workload can overwhelm the capacity of the available adult population, students represent a hidden resource.

Rural residents' shared belief in the value of community and place provides the starting point for the CDP process. Individuals choose to live in a small, rural community because there is something they value about that particular place. They may value the environ-ment, the people, the isolation, the opportunity to be self-sufficient, the small size, or a combination of these factors. Whatever the reasons, place and recognition of what that place has come to mean to them provide the common ground for uniting the community in action. The CDP model incorporates a vision- and consensus-building strategy designed to unite the community. Actively involving students in these activities helps them strengthen their rural identities and develop skills they will need to be effective members of their community.

The CDP process begins with a readiness session meant to assess the level of support from community leaders for community/school development. Once a group of community leaders agrees to sponsor the CDP project, they select a process coordinator and establish deadlines for completing the events in the model.

High school students from the Powder River County High School were involved in the CDP project from its inception. In addition, both elementary and high school teachers participated in all aspects of the project. Program evaluation data show that teacher or other significant adult participation was essential for the sustained involvement of students. This was especially true in terms of incentives such as making projects part of course objectives, offering school credit, using in-school time, and providing the encouragement and guidance necessary for students to follow their own ideas to completion.

Broadus's Progress in Community-School Partnering

Table 3 provides an overview of the events, dates, people involved, and outcomes in the Broadus CDP process. About 45 people attended the first town meeting. The number doubled for the second town meeting and included more high school students. A student leader, who participated in this meeting, led junior- and senior-level students through the same activities presented in Town Meeting 2–vision development and goal setting.

By the time Town Meeting 4 was held, task force groups had carried out short-range information gathering, and developed long-range plans (see Appendix B for a list of task force goals, and student and educator membership). The Broadus community received an $8,000 grant from the local Coal Board as a result of student testimony regarding the impact of student involvement on community development. This grant was used to continue work on redesigning Broadus, and was coordinated by the local art teacher and the county extension agent. A local artist-in-residence also helped students produce a town mural and sculpture.

Table 3. CDP Progress Chart for Broadus, Montana

Key Events	Date/Responsible Parties	Outcomes
Readiness: Conduct initial orientation and obtain agreement to participate	February 1991 Acting process coordinator and NWREL project coordinator	School board resolution and letters of support from key leaders
Event 1: Select process coordinator	February 1991 Community leaders and acting process coordinator	County extension agent assumes the role of process coordinator.
Event 2: Attend process coordinator training (3 days in Portland, OR)	August 1991 Process coordinator, district superintendent, and NWREL project coordinator	Learn group facilitation and leadership skills; develop implementation plans.
Event 3: Conduct community meeting 1	January 1992 Process coordinator and NWREL project coordinator	This was the first community meeting. Forty-five people attended the session. One student was recruited to participate. Community development process was introduced and community council selected.
Event 4: Convene community council	March 1992 Process coordinator and the school district superintendent	Orientation and training was completed for community council.
Event 5: Provide community council training and planning	May 1992 Process coordinator and NWREL project coordinator	A cross-section of the community (including a student) is trained in facilitation skills, interviewing techniques, and how they will help implement the project.
Event 6: Conduct community meeting 2 for vision development and goal setting	September 1992 Process coordinator, community council members, and NWREL project coordinator	Eighty-five residents, including three students, develop a vision for the community and goals for achieving their vision.
Event 7: Conduct community council planning session for community meeting 3	October 1992 Process coordinator, community council members, and NWREL project coordinator	Council is briefed on their facilitator roles for community meeting 3 and involved in decisions about various aspects of the community meeting.

(continued)

Table 3 (continued)

Key Events	Date/Responsible Parties	Outcomes
Event 8: Conduct community meeting 3 for community/ school analysis and action planning	October 1992 Process coordinator, community council members, and NWREL project coordinator	About 80 adults and 8 students attended community meeting 3 and produced 11 short-term action plans, one for each goal. About 23 junior and senior class members completed the visioning activity.
Event 9: Convene community council planning session	October 1992 Process coordinator	A debriefing and training session was held with council to discuss concerns, address needs, and enhance small group facilitation skills. A second meeting was held in which each task force was given the task of completing a long-range plan and presentation for community meeting 4.
Event 10: Conduct community meeting 4 for evaluating progress and long-range planning	February 2, 1993 Process coordinator, community council members, and NWREL project coordinator	More than 75 people representing nine task forces presented their long-range plans for community review. Posters, plans, and models built by students of desired facilities and scale drawings of the community as a frontier town were displayed. Community feedback was incorporated into draft plans, and a final long-range community development plan was completed.

The education task force worked with school officials to implement a course on rural development in the high school and a program for students to shadow employers for a day. In addition, a cross-age tutoring program grew from the interests of a primary teacher who requested high school students be given credit for working with her students. In both the career shadowing and tutoring programs, students helped design the program and presented their plans to the school board for approval.

Student Involvement and Workplace Competencies

How do students perceive the benefits and challenges of their involvement? How has the community and school benefited? How are students better prepared to enter the workforce? The Broadus community and school district had previously placed no more emphasis on school-to-work transition than any other rural school in the state, or perhaps the nation.

As can be seen in Table 3 (outcomes section, events 3, 6, 8 and 9), student involvement increased over time. Initially, only one student appeared to have the time and interest to participate. However, the number of students began to increase as goals developed around their interests. Interestingly, the students who became directly involved reflected a cross-section of career aspirations, from the college bound to those with no clear idea of what they would do after high school.

Teacher involvement also tended to facilitate student interest and participation. For example, after community meeting 2 (event 6), citizens created a vision of what they desired their community to be like in five years. A high school senior, with the support of the social studies teacher, facilitated the development of a student vision for the future. Based upon this student's interest, the entire senior class be- came involved.

The high school principal and the social studies teacher said they had never seen the senior class as motivated and on task. In part, they attributed this motivation to the active nature of the visioning activity, its having been led by a respected student, and the immediate connec- tion to the students' lives. In an interview conducted by the local newspaper, the student facilitator commented on student motivation and involvement:

> The kids really are interested and involved and are ready to do some projects. [They] went through the same process that was involved in the last Town Meeting [and] we took the seniors clear through it.

From this student visioning activity came a set of goals that nearly matched those of the community. This encouraged students and gave them a sense of confidence. By the last two community meetings, students participated on an equal basis with adults. For example, students facilitated brainstorming and planning sessions, and pre- sented reports to the 80 citizens in attendance at Town Meeting 4. It was the first time that many students were actively involved with adults and presented before a large gathering. Presenting before a large audience, working in teams, facilitating planning, and developing reports are all useful skills for the workplace. Students who master these skills will have a head start on employability.

Out of these initial community meetings emerged a realization that students could be valuable resources in setting goals, developing action plans, and actively participating in community and school development.

The Broadus vocational education curriculum had been a traditional in-school program, with few opportunities for exploration of the local community. There seemed to be a lack of awareness of the occupational resources available in the local area. A similar lack of vision afflicts many small, rural communities. All too often, the curriculum reflects a metropolitan context, causing students to perceive that their rural communities lack even the minimal amenities found in the city. As a result, both teachers and students often become blind to the local resources that are available to them. Further, their criteria for what constitutes a useful community learning resource often excludes the natural environment or local culture and history. For example, analyzing water quality or studying economic historical trends and their impact on the local community can serve as opportunities to learn workplace skills. This is not to say that isolated rural communities have all the resources available in metro areas, but it does suggest that many rural resources that do exist are sorely underused.

Community/School Development Partnership

Many of the processes and activities used in implementing the community/school development partnership served to pull the diverse energies in the community into a unified effort, driven by a common vision. This has led people to see the connections to community development in their various school and community activities, which previously seemed unrelated. For example, students from primary classrooms have often visited a local retirement home on field trips. With the advent of the community/school partnership, such activities are recognized as helping achieve community development goals. Students have become more aware of their community and the needs of its citizens. Another example is the use of a computer program for developing thinking skills. The content of this program, called Talents Unlimited, has shifted toward community-based problem solving. The elementary principal facilitated this shift because he felt teachers were more likely to become involved in community development if they built on existing strengths (e.g., knowledge in how to use software such as Talents Unlimited) rather than taking on a new set of responsibilities.

Many other examples of how community development has provided a basis for building workplace competencies can be found throughout the school district. Students worked with the business teacher to develop a database that included information regarding skills, talents, and volunteers in the community. The English teacher worked with students to produce a one-page newsletter that reports on local meetings, games, and important events. The newsletter is distributed by the publication class to cafes, businesses, and other public gathering places.

The business task force published a directory of local businesses and organizations. Students solicited the participation of community businesses and organizations in the project. This resulted in a publication with more than 35 entries. The supervising teacher said students were amazed at the number of services available in their small, rural community. Students have also been active in improving recycling in the community by helping the task force on civic pride raise money for a cardboard bailer. This project was coordinated with the local grocer and a committee on recycling.

The activities described in the next sections help illustrate how these goals played out in the school and in the community.

Task Force Committee Activity

A core group of eight students served as members of various community development task force groups. Each task force was to develop and implement action plans aimed at reaching community-defined goals. The greatest number of students signed up for the recreation task force, with others choosing to work on the community beautification and education committees. Students and adults received training in group facilitation skills. They recorded group comments and ideas and arrived at decisions through consensus. Students also observed a range of organizational and management skills from community leaders, consultants, and local citizens. More important, they assumed leadership roles such as facilitating problem-solving sessions, recording group ideas, and carrying out responsibilities critical for task completion.

An especially noteworthy example emerged out of the work of the task force on education. A student member pointed out that students could learn a great deal about different professions by spending time in local businesses and organizations while receiving credit. The task force adopted the idea after the student presented it to more than 75 local residents attending a community meeting. During the presentation, the student turned to the task force on business enhancement and told them they would gain much by hosting students for a day. "You know," she said, "if you had us spend a day in your businesses, you might get a full day of free student help." As a result, the school has implemented a student intern program in the high school where students can spend a day in a business or organization of their choice.

The administration worked with students to develop the program and had students present it to the school board. This gave students the opportunity to plan, develop, and present their ideas before a governing body, thus helping them to understand the role of policy and governance in school district organizations.

School Intern Program. The intern program is aimed at freshmen and seniors. Freshman participation is limited to internships available in Broadus. Seniors are allowed to intern in Broadus or surrounding communities. Students investigate a vocational topic that interests them, explain why they wish to participate in the intern program, and develop a set of questions they would like answered during their internship. For example, a senior student interested in radio broadcasting would conduct research on broadcasting, develop several questions, and state why radio broadcasting is important. Because there are no broadcasting studios in Broadus, that student would have to visit Miles City, a community 75 miles away.

This approach to learning about the world of work has often been called "career shadowing" because the intern, like a shadow, unobtrusively spends time with a worker learning what he or she does in the workplace. This approach to career awareness has had a number of benefits for a small, rural community. First, it creates a new awareness about the types of employment available in the community. Second, by focusing positive attention on local businesses and organizations, the program has brought the school and community closer together. One student described how people can work together:

If a group of people put their minds to something, it can be accomplished. We set up all the guidelines and covered all possible angles before we presented the program to the school board. As a result, they approved it willingly.

Moreover, this same student, when asked how she might use the skills she had gained in helping to develop this program, said,

I will apply the same tactics toward gaining this program to any other project I may tackle. The more organized and well-thought-out your material is, the better chance it has.

Community beautification task force. This task force provides another example of how students and the school can serve as valuable resources for community development while students learn work and life skills. In this case, the task force contracted a rural planner and architect, along with several graduate students from a state university, to help redesign the community in ways that would make it more inviting for tourists and residents. Task force members sought the help of teachers and students to participate in a community design project. The local art teacher saw it as an opportunity to involve her students in real-life applications of art principles.

As a result, more than 30 students helped draw pictures of buildings, streets, and parks of a redesigned Broadus. In some cases, the design was rendered as a three-dimensional model. Costs for the planning consultants came from the school, the county commission, service club donations, the city government, and a coal board grant. The coal board decided to fund the project after hearing the impassioned plea of a high school senior who said that, before her involvement in community development, she felt

> Broadus was a dead-end, a place without any hope. Now I feel there is hope, that by working together as a community we can bring about changes to make it a better place to live. To make it a place I could move back to and raise a family.

Students also worked with an artist-in-residence to design and create a sculpture, and to paint a large mural on a local building. The mural and sculpture helped beautify downtown while providing students with experiences of scale drawing and painting in large formats. Both the architect and the artist-in-residence helped students learn about these professions.

Several offshoots of community beautification activity emerged. Students cleaned up a vacant lot and converted it into a park after gaining permission to use land belonging to a local landowner. The school provided release time for a community cleanup that allowed a group of students to concentrate their attention on the vacant lot. Students videotaped the downtown area and drew a scale model of Broadus as an early Western frontier town.

The task force on tourism also sought the help of teachers and students to design postcards and assist with other projects. The school's art teacher has been instrumental in student involvement. The art teacher worked with other teachers on the tourism task force and made student involvement a part of class time and credit.

Broadus County High School Community Development Course

A community development course was established for the 1993-94 school year as an outgrowth of the school's commitment to community development. The course provides a space and time for students and staff to pursue community development goals within the existing structure of the school, and it provides incentives for student involvement by granting course credit for participation. During the interviews, both community development course teachers, who had been actively involved in the CDP project, characterized themselves as being "action types of people." This orientation has resulted in a course unlike any other. One of the teachers characterized students as a "structured implementation force" for community development needs. Students design, build, and carry out projects of interest to themselves, other individuals, and school and community groups. Students are gaining lifelong skills such as planning, time management, interpersonal communication, and problem solving.

Students are given freedom to choose projects they care about, but they also are expected to take on projects that will help the school or the community. At this writing the community development course is in its infancy, covering innovative and emerging curriculum content. The following provides an overview of the types of projects, activities and processes found in the course:

School litter project. Two students monitored the school to determine where most littering took place. They charted their two-week study on a school map and identified the areas where there was the highest concentration of litter. They noticed that the high-litter areas did not have trash cans, so they talked with the custodian about the problem. He told the students he had asked for new trash cans more than a year previously. The students went to the principal, presented their supporting data, and trash cans were ordered immediately. The students monitored the area for two more weeks and noticed a reduction in litter. However, they also concluded that their classmates needed to make more of an effort to pick up after themselves throughout the school.

Student recreation center. The community development project also sought ways to provide more recreational opportunities for youth and adults. Students envisioned a community recreation center within five years. In the interim, they developed a recreation center in the school that would provide a place for students to socialize during and after classes. School administration had already set aside an area for students, but its bare walls and limited activities were uninviting. The community development class took on the project and brainstormed ideas. Class members decided the area needed to be made visually attractive, comfortable, and entertaining. This could be accomplished by painting the room; removing unneeded tables; providing comfortable furnishings; and adding a pool table, video games, and a Foosball table. Students presented a plan to administrators that included their ideas, a time frame for getting them done, resources they would need, and other groups and individuals who could help. To carry out the plan required that partnerships be formed and that responsibilities be spread across the student body. While this helped build ownership among students, it also created a conflict with the student council. Council members had decided to undertake a similar project a year earlier. However, neither the school administration nor the community development class knew of the council's plans. The two student groups worked through the conflict and recognized the need for improved communication. As a result, they assigned members from their respective groups to sit in on each other's meetings.

In their quest to develop a recreation center, students also looked to other schools for ideas. Broadus students discussed the development of recreation opportunities with students from Saco, Montana, an isolated rural community northeast of Broadus (Saco's community development efforts are detailed in a later chapter). Saco students,

---

Short-Term Action Plan

Project Name_____ Date_____

Spokesperson_____ Phone_____

Who else should be involved and what action will you take to involve them?_____
_____

Which other task force groups have a stake and how will you coordinate with them?_____
_____

How much will it cost?_____

What information will be needed to make it happen and how will you obtain it?_____
_____
_____

What are the tasks to be done?	Who will do it?	When will it be done?	What resources are needed?

Figure 2. Short-Term Action Planning Form

teachers, and others succeeded in developing a community recreation center, so Broadus students were eager to learn from the Saco experience. Two students in the community development class developed a firewood business to raise money for a field trip to Saco. The students cut, split, and supplied wood to customers in the community. After they paid transportation and other overhead costs, they placed the remainder of their earnings into a field trip fund.

These students are learning to manage time and resources, to work with the public, and to experience the rewards associated with volunteerism. They are also learning the value of self-initiative and hard work. Students said their firewood sales taught them "to get along with a partner and to work with money" and to manage a business.

Emerging projects. As the community development class gained credibility, project requests flowed in from around the school. For example, students raised doubts about the quality and size of school lunches. Students designed a questionnaire to assess how the student body perceived the lunch program. Data from the survey was used as a basis for discussion with school cooks. The vocational education teacher sought student help in defining community and school needs for use in developing a grant proposal. The home economics teacher sought help in developing a cookbook to commemorate the 75th anniversary of the founding of Broadus.

These examples demonstrate the success of the community development course. However, it was not without challenges. Scheduling students into the class was difficult when there were so many other activities and required courses in the school. This problem was partially resolved by offering community development at the same time as study hall. The 50-minute period, which divides up the school day, posed difficulties for projects that needed sustained periods of time. Coordinating priorities within teacher teams can also be problematic. For example, one of the instructors mentioned that conflict sometimes occurred when each instructor had a different priority for student projects. Commenting on what it is like to team teach, one teacher said, "It is really fortunate that we are good friends."

Cross-Age Tutoring

Several teachers from the elementary school and the high school saw a possible linkage between the two schools that could build a greater sense of community within the school district. The result was the development of a cross-age tutoring program, in which high school students tutor those students in the elementary school and receive credit and training for their involvement. Earlier attempts at cross-age tutoring had not been successful because students received little or no training, no credit, and minimal supervision and feedback. For example, an informal agreement had been made between an elementary and high school teacher for several students to help out in the elementary school. Tutors became bored and unreliable, which eventually ended the informal arrangement.

The current program received support from the high school principal, who had successfully helped operate a similar program at another school. He worked closely with teachers and students to design a program and collaboratively develop a proposal that was subsequently approved by the school board for implementation during the 1993-94 school year. As reported in the local newspaper, "High school students volunteering for the program give up three days of weekly study hall time in exchange for one-quarter semester credit. . . . The tutors receive a monthly evaluation from the supervising teacher as an effort to continually improve the program and their efforts" ("Students involved," 1992, p. 7). Moreover, the high school principal reported, "The program is currently a big success for both the high school tutors and the elementary children."

Clearly defined guidelines and expectations for participants have contributed to the program's success. A contract signed by the student, teacher, and principal specifies credit requirements, student responsibilities, attendance, and consequences for failing to live up to agreed-upon expectations. Teachers learned how to use tutors effectively and developed training activities to facilitate a smooth transition for tutors into the classroom. Tutors learned how to work with young children while gaining insight into the work life of teachers. In this way, students provide authentic assistance while learning valuable workplace skills such as scheduling, working with adult supervisors, acting as a positive role model, and exercising necessary flexibility when working with young children. One tutor described her experience:

> Since I started tutoring, I've been thinking about going into something similar for college. Going up to the elementary school is always a learning experience for me as well as the kids. I learn patience, how to get organized, and how important it is for children to have heroes, or at least someone to look up to.

The big payoff may be a closer working relationship among teachers, administrators, and students, leading to a greater sense of community.

Conclusion

Broadus and the Powder River region of southeastern Montana, like many western rural communities, face hard times. With declining opportunities for employment, rural communities suffer the out-migration of youth, especially those with high school diplomas and postsecondary education. Rural youth often believe they have no choice but to leave. Worse, many believe staying in their rural community signifies failure.

To counter this widely held belief about rural life, youth must learn to see the possibility of spending their lives in their home communities as a positive choice for a fulfilling life and meaningful work. This can be accomplished by providing youth with opportunities to become active, responsible members of a community that works together. In isolated rural communities, participation in community development can offer a rich learning alternative, providing students with experience and the opportunity to develop many of the work and life skills they will find useful throughout their work and personal lives.

Broadus residents did not consciously set out to develop school-to-work strategies when they became involved in community development. They started from the understanding that their community faced difficult economic times, and that unless the school and community worked together, their mutual survival was in jeopardy. This context presented an opportunity to explore ways students and the school could address community needs while meeting the basic academic needs of students.

Interviews conducted with educators, students, and residents indicated widescale support for involving students in community-based learning. More important, there was a nearly unanimous opinion that involving students provided invaluable experiences that would help them prepare for their futures. For example, when asked, "How will your involvement in community development be of benefit five years from now?," one student replied:

> You're learning teamwork. You're learning how to negotiate. You're learning how to talk with people. I mean it's better than anything going on in school because it's hands-on. You learn from your mistakes and you learn from the things that you do right. So it's very educational.

Observations by residents and educators substantiated much of what this student said. For example, one parent felt student involvement helped change the way students relate to their community:

I feel real thrilled with what they have done. The students have been so enthusiastic and they have come up with many ideas of what they would like to do. I just feel like they are able to relate to the community in a better way because of this, and thinking what they can do to better it.

Another resident, who serves on the tourism task force, described how students learned to translate their ideas into visual forms for presentation to the public:

The students drafted their own image. . . . They drafted their own map and layout of what they thought the town of Broadus [might look like in the future]. . . . They drew maps, redesigned streets, made boulevards, and wanted to plant trees just [to] beautify, fix up what we have.

The high school principal described how involving students in real-life planning helps them develop important skills and creates pride in who they are as members of a community:

Students helped plan town improvements. An architect came in and worked with them. They went downtown and said, "Now how could we improve the looks of our town?" and came up with, "We've got really wide streets in our town. We could put a divider in the middle of the street and plant flowers and things like that." I think the students buying into that, being a part of the planning process, that's going to be their pride in their community. They will come back ten years from now and say, "I was one who helped do this."

As many residents of the Broadus area have pointed out, the community and school are just at the beginning of what can be accomplished when parents, students, educators, and the general public work together. The Broadus community received substantial help from their involvement in the CDP project. This raises the issue of whether other rural communities can replicate their experiences without outside intervention. If one stands back and looks at the activities occurring in Broadus, they do not look very different from what happens in many small, rural schools. In many rural schools, students may help out in the local retirement home, clean up their playground, or take on any number of projects. What makes the Broadus experience unusual is the change in everyone's perspective about the important roles students can play in their community. Participants also discovered how much can be learned from community-based experiences. Many of the ideas presented here can be adapted and tried in nearly any rural community or neighborhood.

We asked residents, teachers, and administrators what advice they might have for communities and schools interested in developing community-based experiences that would help students learn more about the work of adults and their communities. Their responses follow:

The Community's Views:
- Have a strategy for identifying and using community resources and talents.
- Have a receptive school board.
- Have sufficient resources, such as money and community expertise.
- Have a community that is supportive of education.

Teachers' Views:
- Provide resources, such as money for travel and time to plan and collaborate.
- Have flexible and supportive administrators.
- Have support from the community.
- Provide rewards and incentives for efforts and successes.
- Create flexible schedules that allow more continuous contact time during class.
- Have a system of accountability for all those involved—teachers, students, administrators, and community.

Administrators' Views:
- Have board and community support.
- Develop a climate that allows risk taking.
- Have effective communication within the school, and between school and community.
- Provide adequate resources, such as time and money.
- Provide training and staff development.
- Develop student involvement.
- Plan out what will be done.
- Be patient.

Many elements in the community and school need attention if efforts such as the one in Broadus are to be sustained over time and replicated elsewhere. All three groups agree that having support, communication, planning, and adequate resources are critical elements of success. In each case study site, these elements were necessary for school-to-work learning experiences to succeed.

Building solid community understanding and involvement are essential if school-to-work learning experiences are to be provided for rural youth. Appendix B provides an overview of the activities youth engaged in as they helped their community. When framed against the type of competencies and workplace skills employers say they need from employees (i.e., SCANS), it was clear that students gained valuable experiences.

CHAPTER 3

Saco, Montana:
Creating the Extraordinary with Kids

Goals

1. Develop an entrepreneurial spirit characterized by adaptability, problem solving, and responsibility.
2. Develop leadership through real-world opportunities.
3. Help students develop the workplace skills and competencies required for the 21st century.

The community of Saco, a remote town in northeast Montana, is home to 250 people. On average, fewer than one person per square mile lives in this high plains region, and visiting a metropolitan area represents a major outing for Saco residents. Glasgow, Montana, population 5,000, is 45 miles east of Saco. Canada is a short drive to the north. Billings, the largest metropolitan city in the state, is about a five-hour drive south. Saco typifies many small, rural farming and ranching communities dotting the western prairies. The Saco School District employs about 40 people, provides educational services to 125 students, and is one of the largest businesses in town. Many other businesses have ceased to exist. The old bank building now serves as a bed and breakfast, and students have converted a car repair shop into a youth recreation center. There are two bars, four churches, a gas station, a grocery store, a liquor store, and a motel. A hardware store can be found two miles outside of town next to an agricultural processing plant. The airport, actually a dirt landing strip in a cow pasture, is 28 miles from Saco in Malta, a town of about 3,500.

Although the school district did not set out to create an organized school-to-work program, the belief that education should prepare students to successfully live and work in the world around them has led to a wide variety of opportunities for youth.

Small, rural schools and communities often have been viewed as being handicapped by their isolation, size, and limited resources and opportunities. In part, this view has grown from the influence urban America has exerted over rural schools and communities. This urban influence among rural people often leads to lowered aspirations and diminished beliefs about their own efficacy. Under creative leadership, rural students can develop an entrepreneurial spirit and sense of pride in who they are as members of a rural community.

Saco School District Superintendent Carl Knudsen and his staff have a vision about student ability and learning that unites them in their efforts to provide a quality education. That vision centers on a belief in students' ability to be confident, self-directed learners. This has been accomplished through an emphasis on problem solving, technology, and learning experiences linking students to the world around them.

The Saco staff provide opportunities for students to participate in more than a dozen clubs, organizations, and extracurricular activities in sports, business, problem solving, and leadership. Moreover, an entrepreneurial spirit exists in the school that says "anything is possible." As a result, students have taken on projects such as building a recreation center, writing grants, running a day-care center, and marketing their computer skills.

Using Technology to Enhance Learning Opportunities

Telecommunications and computer technology represent powerful educational tools for helping to overcome geographic isolation. They also are a means of providing students with learning opportunities previously unavailable to them. However, bringing technology into the school requires a commitment to provide teachers with the tools necessary to build an effective strategy for implementing a quality program. Issues such as staff development, the use of technology in a consistent and productive manner, technical support, and student learning must be addressed.

Preparing for the electronic future. The use of technology in Saco schools is pervasive. It is expanding student and staff learning opportunities. The school district serves as a regional telecommunications center for EDUNET, a computer-based electronic course providing access to accredited correspondence courses throughout the Northwest. In 1992, the National Rural Education Association cited EDUNET as an outstanding program serving the needs of rural schools. The Saco District accepted the award because of its pioneering effort as a regional EDUNET center. In addition, the school serves as a regional center for the Montana Educational Telecommunications Network (MetNet). This system was designed to link all teachers in the state through e-mail and MetNet bulletin boards.

The school library provides a satellite downlink and video facilities where community residents and students have access to most state and higher education library holdings and other telecommunications programming. Moreover, every classroom contains direct electronic access to these resources. This means that teachers have direct access from their classrooms to satellite programming and/or downlinked programs. For example, second grade students take Spanish via a satellite program that is viewed in the classroom on a 27-inch color monitor.

In business and technology classrooms, computers have been networked into learning stations which, in turn, were networked with other computers throughout the school. Teachers and students remain in continuous communication. "This year," noted Superintendent Carl Knudsen, "we have every student K-12 on the network through e-mail, and the teachers are just getting used to messaging students their assignments into their files. Teachers have been training students to carry their disks and to have access in every classroom, automatically."

Knudsen envisions the network creating many more opportunities for teachers to collaborate with one another, to integrate the curriculum, and to better serve student needs. Computer software has been purchased to encourage and facilitate integration. Knudsen believes that technology can encourage "cross-content and team teaching" if the technology is user-friendly and accessible to everyone. "The English teacher has been trying to get the science and math programs to write joint papers across content areas," he said. "But ensuring that papers get passed around can create hassles that hinder integration." However, the schoolwide network and new process-writing software have provided opportunities for students to write an essay in an English class, then e-mail it to the science teacher. "They could also message it on-line and edit it without having to download their paper into a separate word-processing program," Knudsen said.

The school also has a supply of notebook computers that may be checked out by students and parents. These computers provide students who are out of school with a means of keeping up with their school work. Teachers place assignments on computer disks and send them home for students to complete. Completed assignments are returned to school in the same manner.

Technology has become pervasive in Saco schools. "We don't have problems with students forgetting textbooks in their lockers," said one teacher. "Now, they forget their computer disks." This presence of technology drives changes in the Saco schools. Students have become literate about computers, application programs, telecommunications, and a host of other related components. This has boosted student confidence about technology and gives Saco students an edge in the workplace and at college.

"We've turned out students who went to college and actually had to help teach the course," Knudsen said. "We had a student who was so proficient that he was working for the mining company at Boardman doing all the drafting and using school printers. They ended up paying him. In fact, they paid all his college expenses and rented a house for him as long as he would work for them."

School librarian Gary Carmichael provided a glimpse of how technology has positively affected students and helped prepare them for a rapidly changing world where technology plays a major role. "The kids have almost a voracious appetite for knowledge and learning," he said. "There have been days when I had to keep the kids off the CD-ROM because they spent all their time looking up different information. They aren't afraid of the technology. That's the key—not to be afraid of technology and new things."

Extending the walls of the school. Several Hutterite religious colonies exist within the Saco School District. The Hutterites are a religious sect which, in general, does not believe in providing formal education for their children after they reach the age of 16, especially if it means being away from the colony. Hutterite elders are concerned about preserving their agrarian way of life. Attending school is often viewed as compromising Hutterite cultural norms. As young adults, Hutterite children are expected to become active members of the colony, helping with farming and other responsibilities designed to sustain their way of life.

When one Hutterite student attending Saco High School turned 16, she was not allowed to continue school and graduate with her class. Knudsen said the student was highly motivated and wanted to receive a diploma. Ironically, Hutterites at her colony use computers and other technologies to help them manage colony business. With this knowledge in mind, Knudsen and school staff developed a strategy using technology that would allow the student to continue her studies from her home in the colony. Through the use of a computer and a phone modem, the student kept in daily contact with her EDUNET teachers, receiving and returning completed assignments over the phone lines.

Knudsen said this same technology could be used to allow other rural students to continue their high school education without having to attend school daily. "When students use the computer to do a course," Knudsen said, "they're not just learning the subject matter. They're also learning computer skills, keyboarding, software, and data transfer." These are all skills of the contemporary workplace.

Technology has facilitated learning in other ways at Saco School. Consider, for example, the experiences of two students who used EDUNET to extend their learning opportunities. The first student, a boy in the 10th grade, transferred to Saco from another Montana school district where he was having academic and behavior problems. During his interview, the student confided that his previous school was big and that no one really cared whether he passed or failed. "I sat in math class day in and day out, not learning anything," he said. "I failed most of my subjects."

In order to take courses at the appropriate grade level in the larger district, the student would have to retake and pass all the courses he failed, which he viewed as impossible—until he moved to Saco. Through EDUNET, he could take the failed classes via electronic correspondence while attending those courses appropriate to his grade level. "Here, people know who I am and care about me," the student said. "Even the superintendent knows my name, stops to ask how I'm doing. At one time, he held a meeting with teachers and me to see how they could help me get back on track. That would never happen at my previous school."

The second student was a senior. Her goal was to graduate, get married, and open a day-care program in the community. She was interviewed while sitting in front of a computer taking a course on child development. She said she had taken all the courses offered in the home economics program and had turned to EDUNET to gain additional knowledge on opening and operating a day-care center.

In observing her with the computer and asking her questions about how the system operated, it was clear that her knowledge of computers and technology was quite advanced. Not only was she gaining knowledge about early childhood education, she was also learning valuable technological work skills that may be of use when she opens her day-care facility.

    Service as a resource for the community. During interviews, several examples emerged of how students use technology to provide service to the community. For example, students have used computers to help cartographers do scale drawings of the county. Students also have taught evening computer courses for the community. The community library and the school library have been electronically connected, thus providing community access to the school's information holdings, while broadening the resources available to the school.

    Dwight Freeman, a technology teacher, said students have surpassed his wildest expectation with technology and problem solving: "They're asking me questions and I don't know the answers," he said. "They have pushed me with the computers. In a way, it's really nice for kids to see teachers learning with them because that is a model of

Table 4. Sources of Funding for Innovation at the Saco School District

Funding Source	Grantee	Purpose of Grant
Star Schools Program grants	Competitive grant awarded to the Saco Public Schools	Provided hardware, interactive video courses in Spanish and Russian, and professional development opportunities for teachers.
State Carl Perkins Vocational Allocation Grants	Competitive grant awarded to the Computer-Assisted Vocational Guidance Consortium	Twenty-six schools received training, one or more computers, and Discovery vocational software. Saco serves as the host district. Saco teachers use all training computers and software, and provide leadership to other schools.
State Vocational Allocation Grants	Competitive grant awarded to the Saco Public Schools	Grants helped fund equipment, travel, and expenses for student organizations to participate in local, state, and national meetings and activities.
State Eisenhower Math and Science Program	Competitive grant awarded to the Northeastern Montana Curriculum Consortia	Saco served as host district, administering funds and hosting curriculum and staff development in the areas of science and math education.
State Chapter 2	Competitive grant awarded to the Northeastern Montana Curriculum Consortia	Saco served as the host district. Grant funded school improvement and staff development activities.

lifelong learning. I had a mind-set of what they would and wouldn't be able to do, and they've blown that right out of the water."

These state-of-the-art technologies cost money and require ongoing maintenance. Learning to effectively use computers also requires extensive staff development. Knudsen has been masterful at seizing opportunities for bringing in additional revenues to the district, especially those that support technology and teacher training. Nearly all staff development and new technologies have been funded from resources outside the general operating budget. This has resulted in freeing local funds for such needs as building and maintenance. Table 4 provides an overview of additional funding and its targeted purposes from 1988 through 1994. During this time, the district has brought in $2.5 million in additional resources.

Table 4 (continued)

Funding Source	Grantee	Purpose of Grant
National Rural Electric Association	Competitive grant awarded to FOCUS (Fiber Optic Consortia for Uniting Schools)	Money was used to network consortia schools with fiber optic cable and provide educational and medical benefits to rural communities.
State Carl Perkins Home Economic Funds	Competitive grant awarded to the Saco Public Schools	Remodeled home economics room into a Family and Consumer Science facility.
Serve America Program	Competitive grant awarded to the Saco Public Schools	Students wrote and received funding for developing a youth recreation center.
State Talented and Gifted Appropriations	Competitive grant awarded to the Saco Public Schools	Provided training for teachers in gifted and talented program development. Also provided for software and curriculum materials to extend existing efforts.
State Drug and Alcohol Prevention Grant	Competitive grant awarded to the Saco Public Schools	Grant provided computer courseware, curriculum, and training in drug-prevention-related areas such as team building, leadership, etc.
State Energy Conservation Grants	Competitive grant awarded to the Saco Public Schools	Grant helped to upgrade heating systems to make them more energy efficient.

Surviving the high cost of technological innovation. It could be argued that relying on external funding develops a dependency in a small district that could create serious problems once the funding declines. Knudsen addressed this concern.

As shown in Table 4, much of the money has been used to build local capacity and infrastructure, not only in Saco, but throughout Northeast Montana. For example, FOCUS represents a consortia of rural communities installing fiberoptic cable in order to link their schools and communities and to connect them with information sources available through the Internet and other telecommunications resources. As a result, adult education programming will become available to health and other service providers.

The Computer-Assisted Vocational Guidance Consortium provides training and hardware to expand career exploration options for students. Many of the smaller school districts, Knudsen says, would not normally seek this money because the revenue gained does not justify the effort or paperwork required to complete the grant. For example, the smallest schools could receive a maximum $104 as a single grantee. The consortia, though, provides much more: a computer, training, and software.

Knudsen has had the foresight to build in strategies that would help the district survive a transition to a new superintendent and a reduction in revenues. Staff has been hired and trained with an eye toward assuming administrative leadership in the future. The teaching principal is getting a superintendent's credential and learning to write grants. The English teacher is helping the superintendent write district policy. The district also hired an accountant who previously owned and managed a computer store, thus providing staff expertise for servicing and maintaining technology. Lastly, by participating in a series of consortia, the superintendent has created infrastructure for the district that ensures opportunities for curriculum and staff development, ongoing vocational and career options for students, and access to telecommunications.

Using Extracurricular Activities to Extend Learning

Most rural schools provide extracurricular opportunities for students, but at Saco the offerings have become a key strategy for extending curriculum. Table 5 provides an overview of the various clubs and activities available, along with the percentage of students participating in each activity. Not surprisingly, athletics rank at the top. This is typical in rural schools.

To counterbalance this tendency, Knudsen initiated an innovative program whereby the principles of athletic coaching and competition could be used in the academic arena. "We have paid an academic coach at the same level as the athletic director and the basketball coach," Knudsen says. "The academic coach organizes and directs teams for the Academic Olympics, the Science of Olympiad, and the Science Fair, including the submission of all application materials." Knudsen notes that a stipend is paid to every extracurricular advisor as well. "Academic advisors work countless hours for academics," he says.

What drives the emphasis on clubs and organizations is the belief that students need to broaden their experiences beyond their community if they are to have the work-related and social skills necessary as adults living in either rural or urban settings. Because of their limited direct exposure to a predominantly urban society and work environment, rural students often see themselves as second-class citizens, which can lead to diminished aspirations. To be competitive in the world of work, rural students need exposure and experiences that will help them navigate the complexities of the world outside their communities.

In Saco, students participate in more than 50 club- and organization-related field trips including state and national conventions, music festivals, junior- and senior-high academic competitions, and training programs for working with peers.

Clubs and related experiences provide opportunities for rural students to test their perceptions and talents among other rural and nonrural students. Only 3 percent of the student body (2 students out of 64) did not participate in any extracurricular activities. Clearly, the vast majority (97 percent) participate, with more than 16 percent involved in three or more activities. When those interviewed were asked if these extracurricular activities were producing positive outcomes for students, they answered with a unanimous "yes."

"In the last couple of years, our business professional students have gone to the nationals," noted an employee of the school who also is a parent. "One of them hit fourth place, and these are from thousands of kids from all over the United States." Just qualifying for the national competition is difficult, according to teaching principal Larry Crowder. "In order to qualify for the nationals, you have to be among the three highest-achieving students in the state." Students also have received recognition as office holders at the regional and state levels in the Technology Students Association (TSA) and Future Homemakers of America (FHA).

Table 5. Percentage of Students Who Participate in School Organizations

Rank	Activity	Percent
1	Basketball	64
2	Band	52
3	Track	31
4	Future Homemakers of America (FHA)	27
5	Business Professionals of America (BPA)	25
6	Student Council	25
7	Technology Student Association (TSA)	23
8	Pep Club	23
9	Science of Olympiad	17
10	National Honor Society	16
11	Academic Team	16
12	Cheerleading	14
13	Play	13
14	Odyssey of the Mind	11
15	Students Trying To Understand Drugs	8
16	Speech and Drama	8

Respondents also said that students were gaining skills that would prepare them for the world of work and adulthood. Skills mentioned included grant writing, negotiating, presentation skills, conflict management, problem solving, and written and oral communications. Stacie Fladland, a senior student and president of TSA, believes club activities have provided real-life opportunities for applying what she has learned in school. This is especially true of her involvement in creating a youth recreational center, where she and other students have employed accounting, interviewing, computer, and business skills. "We use these skills when we call businesses and ask for donations or request someone to come in and check the electricity," she said. "There's woodworking skills, English, everything will be used."

Making Learning Relevant to Students' Needs

Saco staff have worked hard to make learning experiences address the needs of their rural, isolated community. Clubs and field trips have exposed students to the world around them, and academic courses also include a "real-world" application. Technology has ensured that students have access to a wide range of curriculum—Russian and Spanish, for example, are not usually found in small, rural communities. Technology also has provided modems, notebook computers, and electronic correspondence, which permit students to complete academic requirements away from the physical structure of the school. This exposure to technology has provided students up-to-date information about office automation such as electronic accounting, spreadsheets, page layout programs, and databases. In vocational art classes, students have become proficient enough in Autocad and related graphics programs to teach their teachers.

Youth recreation center as curriculum. Youth in small, isolated rural communities often need a place to gather and socialize at times when the school is unavailable. In metropolitan areas, young people generally have a variety of recreational options such as the YMCA and YWCA, private health clubs, and park and recreation programs. Because of low population density and its accompanying small tax base, these opportunities are limited or unavailable in rural areas.

In Saco, there are no places for youth to gather on weekends and during the evenings except the local bars. "We go there with our parents, but sometimes we just go in there and play pool," a senior student said. Although school-age youth are underage, they have been allowed to play pool and listen to music since there is no other place to gather and socialize. "They are kind of lenient to our being in the bars because that is the only place we have to go after 6:30 at night," noted another student. "That's the only thing that's open downtown. If we can open a recreation center, then the town can enforce the laws and quit being so lenient."

Students and Knudsen discussed the idea of developing a youth recreation center. Knudsen told students of a possible location for their recreation center, but added that the students needed to initiate and carry out their proposal. "You have to meet those people who own it," he said. "If you want this, it has to be your effort because it will only be successful if you want it to be." Knudsen and the school staff did not just drop the ball on students and tell them to go for it. They provided ongoing guidance and support over several years. As a result, students have created a youth recreation center that officially opened in 1994. Table 6 presents the sequence of events and activities that led to the opening of the recreation center.

The development of the recreation center illustrates learning in a real-world context while simultaneously addressing school curriculum goals. The recreation center project also represents ways to capitalize on an opportunity for developing school-to-work skills in an isolated, rural setting. Interview data reveal rich opportunities for youth to learn valuable work and life skills. When asked what they were learning, students demonstrated a sophisticated grasp of how their academic courses applied to their recreation center work. For example, Stacie Fladland, chairperson of the student recreation board, said she used English, public speaking, journalism, and other skills. Another student said she learned to conduct interviews, write job resumes, raise money, and keep the books. "You've got to make decisions of whether you should buy this or that, and what you shouldn't buy," she said.

Students also learned many practical lessons, such as negotiating a lease on property, borrowing money from the bank, and making sure property was insured. In addition, they learned interior decorating, wiring, plumbing, and other design and remodeling skills. Workplace experiences occurred because school staff held high expectations that

Table 6. The Sequence of Events, Adult Support, and Student Learning in the Development of a Youth Recreation Center

Events	Adult Support	What Students are Learning
Students discuss with superintendent the idea of a youth center.	Superintendent describes needed actions, mentions town building they may want to inspect, and suggests a grant to get money.	How to work through bureaucracy to achieve desired goals using problem analysis and planning
Students conduct survey.	Sponsors suggest finding out how much support exists for the recreation center.	Survey research, building support, and identifying participants
Students form a recreation center board; write two grants.	Vocational club sponsors (BPA, FHA, and TSA), the principal, and the superintendent help interpret grant guidelines and coach students.	Cooperation, management, leadership, grant writing, and goal setting and planning
Parent advisory board formed.	Advice and encouragement from sponsors.	Importance of having support from key constituents
Student board defines needs and investigates options.	Students guided through the issues to consider, people to visit, and actions to consider.	Problem analysis, planning, negotiations, and public speaking
Students present their grant proposal to the school board.	Board approves proposal and provides 30 percent matching funds.	Organization and presentation skills; how bureaucracy operates and who has power

students could take charge of the recreation center project, provided they were given adequate support. "The kids have done everything," said Dwight Freeman, a club sponsor.

"We give our suggestions when they get stuck or in a bind, but they make the decisions. They have had to deal with the owner of the building, which wasn't always easy. That was a good learning experience for them. They're in charge of the remodeling and overseeing its completion." Like students, staff have learned much from the recreation center project. They have learned the importance of giving decision-making power to students and trusting that they will carry out a plan. They also learned that an entire community will support a project when it reflects a local need and draws upon local skills and strengths.

Table 6 (continued)

Events	Adult Support	What Students are Learning
Grants funded; students negotiate building with lease-buy option.	Sponsors and administration work with the student board to lay out tasks and timelines.	What is involved in leasing a building, borrowing money, getting insurance, utilities cost, etc.
Students clean building.	Sponsors and parents supervise and open building on weekends.	Coordination, value of ownership and hard work, and managing time
Drafting students draw up remodeling plan; home economic students develop decorating plan.	Home economics and technology teachers integrate recreation remodeling activities into their courses.	Application of academics and technology to real-life situations; planning, designing, and working together for common purpose
Student board expanded.	Club sponsors discuss ways to make student board stronger.	How to build an organizational structure that can be sustained over time
Center opened and prom held.	Club sponsors use class time for remodeling. Community volunteers with expertise in sheet rocking, wiring, and plumbing work with students.	Managing volunteers, all phases of remodeling, task analysis and planning, value of hard work
Students remodel facility.	Staff, administration, and community celebrate with students.	Building support, planning, and hard work pay off

Students built a support base early on by informing adults of their goals, seeking their active involvement, and demonstrating their interest through hard work and enthusiasm. For example, students worked after school and on weekends, when they also persuaded community volunteers to chaperone their remodeling activities. When residents saw that students were working long, hard hours on the project, they committed to it as well. To be sure, there were skeptics. But students kept pressure on teachers and the community to be involved. Students recognized an important concept of successful change: desired outcomes require consistent group effort and support. This understanding reflects Fladland's observation regarding her growth as a leader. "You're always trying to keep yourself motivated to keep going," she says. "There's always something to do, and you've got to keep on your toes to make sure it gets done."

Freeman has been surprised at the success of the project. During the early phase, sponsors and administrators kept pressure on students to stay involved. But once the actual remodeling began, students kicked into high gear. "High school and junior high students began to think this is really going to work,'" Freeman said. "The rec center might actually happen." From that point on, students moved into the driver's seat.

Freeman and other sponsors made another critical decision that boosted student participation in the project. They integrated the remodeling into existing curricula, thus using class time to work on the recreation center. The decision reflected another reality of life in small, rural communities: Students and staff get stretched thin from the variety of activities they are involved in, and burnout becomes a problem. According to one student, when the project became part of class time, involvement jumped to nearly 75 percent of the student body. Involvement became contagious, Freeman said:

> At first it was just one of my classes, but as we started having work sessions, people would observe the activity and think, "Hmm, maybe we can go in there. Let's go see what they're doing." One day Curtis Schultz went in the center while they were taping sheetrock. He had never taken any type of shop or vocational course before. He had never taped before. Someone said, "Want to learn how?" He said, "Sure." They just took him to a wall and started teaching him how to tape.

Moreover, involvement went beyond students. The community, especially skilled laborers such as electricians, plumbers, and sheet rockers, volunteered time. Students would call an electrician, for example, explain the recreation center project, and then ask for help. "We told them basically what they had to teach, what it was for, and asked if they would be willing to help us," Freeman said. "They all said yes. I was flabbergasted."

The recreation center held a grand opening in the fall of 1994. "I was shocked," Freeman said. "That first night we earned $50. Now, when the place is open, there are kids in there, anywhere from 5th graders through seniors. The seniors are playing [a card game]. It's a big thing."

However, the student recreation board has had to make tough decisions regarding expenditures and supervision. "We have a long way to go and we all have a lot to learn," Freeman said. Among the considerations: Should the center sell food in competition with the local cafe? Should a new heating system be installed, increasing center debt? Should the telephone be removed to save money? How should potential supervisors be screened? And most important, how does the center remain open if expenditures are greater than revenues? These problems provide significant opportunities for students to become productive members of their community. In so doing, they create learning experiences truly reflecting the real world. What better preparation can there be for the world of work than students problem solving, planning, setting goals, and making decisions in collaboration with their peers and adults?

Freeman's technology program: transforming the purposes of learning. In 1985, Freeman got a wake-up call from Superintendent Knudsen. "Dwight, your job is endangered," Knudsen told Freeman. "You need to recruit students. You need to offer students what they want, not what you want to teach."

Freeman had been a traditional vocational education and shop instructor, teaching courses in small engines, woodworking, and metal working. "Enrollment dropped to where my class load was down to eight students in a semester," Freeman said. "Students didn't want to take small engines or woodworking." Freeman sensed that something was wrong:

> I was getting bored. It was the same book I learned in college. I knew the book inside and out. I knew where the kids were in the book. I could answer the questions automatically. I always wanted 100 percent control of my class. You do it my way or no way at all. The kids were just robots.

Freeman changed. He gave students the opportunity to decide what they wanted to learn; they set their own goals and planned a course of action. As a result, Freeman's classes changed. For example, he blended his woodworking, small engine, and metal working classes into a single class. "I did away with product orientation such as building a table in shop class," Freeman said. "I moved toward a problem-solving orientation where students learned to apply their knowledge in settings and through techniques that have come to be seen as important workplace competencies." Students, Freeman said, were now learning skills such as "working in small groups or teams, brainstorming, problem analysis and solution seeking, cooperation with others, information seeking and retrieval, negotiations, leadership roles, and responsibility."

At the heart of this change resides the pivotal concept of using problem solving to help students learn to apply their knowledge. "The number one thing is problem solving, how to incorporate your academics, your math, your science, your history—even P.E." Freeman said. "It is actually using knowledge by thinking out a problem." From this transformation in teaching style, Freeman developed a course on applied technology, K-12. He defines technology as "using all your other academic courses in an application form, using a problem-solving approach. Technology isn't all the fancy equipment and learning how to use it. It is kids learning to think in a progressive manner. It's learning through direct hands-on experience."

Freeman teaches technology at all grade levels. Curriculum grows from the content of the class and is collaboratively planned with each teacher. For example, in the first grade, students were studying about outer space and the need to work together. "Students built a space shuttle and they had to work together," Freeman said. "They had to be inside the shuttle with each student having one arm out, working the two arms together to pick up objects. They could not see what the other hand was doing. Boy, if that doesn't get them trying to work together."

In the fifth-grade class, students were introduced to the role trees play in paper production and learned the value of recycling. Students placed boxes throughout the school and collected, sorted, and weighed the paper. They estimated the amount of paper thrown away in the school. Students also conducted an information campaign about recycling. Freeman introduced students to computer-assisted drawing, and they created posters and decorated their recycling boxes. Freeman believes students gain a greater understanding for the purposes of learning when they connect academics to real-life applications.

Home economics. Home economics has provided other real-life learning opportunities for students. Home economics students learned about interior design and decorating when they worked on the recreation center project. Students have participated in other noteworthy activities to apply their knowledge. For example, they cooked and served lunches for a series of community information meetings organized by the superintendent. Student grades were based on their performance across a range of competencies associated with operating and working in a restaurant.

On another occasion, students set up a day-care program for the community. The program was supervised by a teacher but operated by students in the school. As a result, one student has taken additional early childhood courses on EDUNET and plans on opening a child-care center upon graduation. Students interested in working with younger children can also work as teaching interns and volunteers in the elementary school. Knudsen said such activities promote career exploration. Interestingly, the third grade teacher acquired her interest in teaching while participating in such a program when she was a student at Saco High School.

The home economics program has been developed around the interests and needs of students. Student interest and staff understanding of student needs define what will be taught. The textbook and other resources are tools available to students, but they do not determine their education program. Knudsen said this instructional approach is "individualized, so that some students in the same class could be sewing, some could be doing nutritional things, and some could be doing family planning and child care."

Such innovative strategies are not without their problems. For example, the home economics teacher complained because she had students from seventh grade to senior level. This created frustrations that Knudsen and the teacher worked out:

> All of a sudden the two older girls said, "We already learned that; we learned that last year, we learned that the year before. We learned all of this stuff." The teacher was frustrated. I suggested that she have the two students who know everything teach the ones that don't and grade them for their productivity. A few days later, the teacher came into my office and said, "I can't believe it, those kids are working hard; they're presenting and they're using good strategies."

Such instructional flexibility and leadership are hallmarks of the promising school-to-work practices found at the Saco School.

Conclusion

How students learn about the world of work is at least as important as the content they learn. In the traditional approach described by Freeman, students focused on teacher-defined learning tasks such as welding tubing into a car frame, cooking a full-course meal, or building a set of bookcases. In the approach currently emphasized at Saco, learning has shifted away from teacher-directed content and abstracted textbook-based curriculum. Learning experiences have become more contextualized, more student-directed and controlled. Students learn higher-order thinking skills and strategies, problem-solving approaches, how to set goals, and how to find and retrieve information by engaging in "real" situations where they assume responsibility for their own learning. In other words, students develop their capacity to learn how to learn (see Table 7).

Small, rural schools and communities can do much to help youth develop the competencies and skills necessary for being happy and productive citizens. Because of their size, they have greater flexibility than schools in metropolitan areas. And although there are fewer occupational choices and experiences, there is a much higher level of student involvement than that found in larger schools. Lastly, there tends to be an intimacy in small places. People know and look out for one another. These characteristics of small, rural communities are valuable assets in overcoming the constraints that isolation and small size impose. The Saco community and school system implemented an educational philosophy that built upon these rural strengths.

Although they do not have a traditional, well-articulated school-to-work program, their vision of what learning should accomplish for students has produced instructional practices well worth considering. Saco educators and others in the community have transformed their small, rural school into a showcase for others seeking ways to prepare youth for adulthood.

Table 7. Dimensions of the Ideal Learning Environment

Learning Dimension	Description	School-Based Illustration
Content or knowledge	Refers to the content, strategies, and procedures specific to a domain or subject such as history, writing, photography, or cooking.	Freeman used problem solving as a means for applying knowledge to real world situations. He called this process of application *technology* (e.g., 5th grade students developing recycling around a unit on trees).
Instruction or learning methodology	Refers to the work relationship between student and teacher, their roles, and responsibilities. Also included are principles that make visible and accessible to the teacher "the reasoning, knowledge, and strategies that students bring to their problem solving (p. 393)."	The teacher's role is redefined to take on (1) modeling what is to be learned by actually doing (e.g., actually writing with students); (2) coaching by observing students during tasks, offering support, feedback, and hints; and (3) organizing learning to help students externalize their thought processes and compare them to others (e.g., knowledge, reasoning, and problem solving).
Sequencing and orchestrating knowledge and events	This dimension addresses the importance of when certain types of knowledge are to be learned and in what context. The focus is on how best to deepen knowledge in order to increase student expertise.	Students were supported by expert staff in planning, writing, and implementing the recreation grants. A process of expert support was used throughout. Students met with bankers, negotiated a building lease, and learned to wire and tape sheet rock.
Social context of learning	Learning should be in an authentic, real context where the learning situation reproduces characteristics of the real world: technology, social relationships, incentives, and time frame.	Saco students actively participated in remodeling an old building into a recreation center. The center became the context within which they applied academic knowledge: grant writing, goal setting, interior design, Autocad plans, and collaborative planning across the school vocational clubs and classes.

(adapted from Berryman, 1993, p. 392-393)

CHAPTER 4

Methow Valley, Washington: Community as Classroom

Goals

1. Help students leave high school with real-world experiences and academic skills that will prepare them for the world of work, whether that means going to college, becoming an auto mechanic, or attending a trade school.

2. Have students work with mentors and models in the community who can show how they live and work to accomplish important goals.

Liberty Bell High School is located between the towns of Twisp and Winthrop in the Methow Valley, a 50-mile scenic corridor that follows the Methow River through the north-central Cascades in Washington State. Surrounded by mountains, the Methow Valley provides a haven for those who love outdoor recreation. The nearest sizable town is Wenatchee, a two-hour drive from the school district offices in Winthrop.

The school district is remote, rural, and has low population density. Residents reflect four general groups: (1) longtime residents whose livelihoods revolve around resource-dependent work such as mining, logging, and agriculture; (2) alternative life-style seekers who have left urban areas for the rural, natural environment; (3) destination resort/tourism entrepreneurs; and (4) retirees. In recent years the valley's economy has shifted toward tourism and service-related industries. In addition, the resource extraction and tourism industries have created an uneven economic picture, with a boom-and-bust business cycle. The school district provides the most steady employment and, with little teacher turnover, some of the highest-paid work in the valley.

Origin and Focus of School-to-Work Programming

The Methow School District and community received a Washington State 21st Century Schools grant in 1990 to restructure the educational program and bring the community in as an active partner with the schools through the creation of community-based instructional activities taught by residents. Out of this initial work emerged Methow Valley as a Classroom (MVCR) and a comprehensive strategic plan within which new and future grants and activities were to be (and have been) integrated. Federal School-to-Work (STW) funds have been used to extend the original reform effort. Currently the STW program comprises 14 components:

1. Methow Valley as a Classroom (MVCR)
2. Diversified Occupations program (DO)
3. Community Resource Training program (CRT)
4. Courses in computers and technology
5. Personal Choices (a freshman course addressing applied communications such as personal decision making and career choices)
6. Independent Living (a senior level course that addresses applied communications such as resume writing, job interviews, and income tax preparation)
7. Expanded offerings through a Tech Prep Consortium
8. Block scheduling to create time for project and community-based activities
9. Pathways to Academic and Career Success (a program beginning in the freshman year that helps students think about and plan their career choices)
10. Washington Occupational Information System (WOIS) beginning at grade 6
11. Expedition Methow (a 7th- and 8th-grade course designed to help students better understand and appreciate the natural environment of the Methow Valley)

12. Running Start (a program through Wenatchee Valley College that provides college-level programming to high school students)

13. A lifelong learning strand woven into the physical education program

14. An occupational trades strand

The central component of school-to-work activities—the primary focus of this chapter—is the Methow Valley as a Classroom program. This program offers more than 200 community-based learning experiences to students in grades 9 through 12 (see Table 8 for a sample of the activities). Since school-to-work activities are predominantly community based, a high level of support exists among constituent groups in the community, including educational organizations such as the Tech Prep program at Wenatchee Valley Community College.

The district has charted a course toward making the entire educational enterprise serve the postsecondary needs of students. Methow Valley as a Classroom, Diversified Occupations, Community Resource Training, and the academic program continue to provide the basic structure for Methow Valley's STW program. However, combined with the other components listed above, the STW program is well articulated to meet the diverse needs of all students within the rural context of the Methow Valley. Expedition Methow, for example, provides a quarter-long enrichment class that helps students appreciate the place where they live by making the local environment the focus of study. A school staff person, with the help of more than 20 community instructors, teaches the course.

The rural context is often overlooked by officials from nonrural areas and colleges, who tend to define STW programming in terms of specialized, high-tech job opportunities available in urban settings. As the superintendent and members of the vocational advisory committee pointed out in interviews, "The Valley is growing and the need for individuals skilled in the trades is greater than ever, and not every student wants to go to college. Many students would stay in the Valley if they could find employment."

Program Components

Given the rural character of the Methow School District, the STW program does not have the broad base of a traditionally articulated program of career, vocational, and academic courses. However, with the implementation of a career pathways and portfolio information program, the district has managed to articulate the diversity of community and school resources available in the Valley—no small feat for an isolated rural school district. Also, this program seems to do much more than prepare youth for a career. Youth and adults concur that students also develop an appreciation for the community, its culture, and the place called the Methow Valley.

A for-credit strand of vocational choices is housed within the academic program of the school, which means that *all* students, including those in the college prep program, take three vocational courses. A new trades strand, Technology Education, allows students to take applied courses in woods and metals, where they practice such advanced skills as computer-aided drafting and project management. This program came on line with the completion of the Methow Valley's new high school and the hiring of a trades instructor. Before the district's STW program was initiated, the small school offered nonacademic electives in only four areas: business, home economics, shop, and art/music. MVCR enhances the district's more traditional credit options, and represents an unusual and effective way to expand student opportunities for career exploration.

Methow Valley as a Classroom. As the central component of the district's STW program, Methow Valley as a Classroom (MVCR) allows students to participate in community-based learning experiences that fall into four strands: (1) career and jobs skills classes, (2) informational classes, (3) community service, and (4) leisure and recreational time activities. Courses are taught by community instructors from local businesses, government agencies, and community groups as well as individuals with expertise in areas of interest to students. To gain an appreciation for the extensiveness of the community's involvement in this program, see Table 8, which lists a portion of the more than 200 offerings to students.

Ten objectives provide a focus for the program:

· Build a relationship between school and community.
· Introduce high school students to local job opportunities.
· Acquaint high school students with local talents.
· Involve high school students in leisure activities in the Methow Valley.
· Involve high school students in service within the community.
· Expose high school students to a full-day experience.
· Provide the opportunity for older people to get to know school teenagers.

(continued, page 63)

Table 8. Methow Valley as a Classroom—Selected Offerings

Curriculum Strands: Career and job skills classes; informational classes; community service; and leisure and recreational activities

Career and Job Skills Classes

Aero Methow Rescue: Be on call and work on construction with Larry Higbee while waiting for a call.

Architects and Drafting: Learn from Howard Cherrington.

Automotive:
RSI—Work with Mike Port
Kevin Collision—Work with Kevin Hickman
Bair Body Shop—Work with Gene Bair
Methow Valley Repair—Work with Larry Smith
Coyote Ridge—Work with Gary Clark

Bear Creek Lumber: Work in the office and on the computer doing data entry and light typing. Debbie Francis says she will make it as fun as possible. Experience the international trade of lumber from Claud and Ella Bannick & Co.

Cascade Concrete: Larry Patterson is willing to show you how concrete is made and how items are made of concrete—septic tanks, well rings, cattle guard bases, and varied pads. View the rock crusher, washing and screening of sand (4 different kinds and gravel), and help pour cement. Wear clothes that can get dirty, and heavy shoes.

Chiropractor: Learn from Drs. Mark and Jody Love. You will be able to spend time working with patients and see how this medical field works. This class is for juniors and seniors.

Contractors: Learn about the world of construction.
Jim Monegan—masonry
Skip Smith—carpentry
Gene Westlund—carpentry
Dan Doran—carpentry

Computer Specialist: Spend time becoming acquainted with the Forest Service computer system, including the word processor. Linda Dulac will assist you.

Computer: Learn programming from Bill Stolberg or Ann George.

Construction, Wood Finish Work: Help complete a wooden staircase by making steps, sanding, staining, and finishing with perfection. Scott Hutchins is a true artistic craftsman in wood finish work.

Dental Assistant: You will learn the different parts of assisting a dentist, work with the hygienist, and see a dentist in action. Kathy Smith will assist you.

Electrical: Tom Sullivan, Jon Francis, Earl Lathrop, or Dwight Filer will share with you their electrical profession. They will take you on their local jobs and you can be a right-hand sidekick.

Food Sales: Hanks Market—Deli, meat, produce, general, video involved with skyline and cable logging and see how these are charged.

(continued)

Table 8 (continued)

Government: Understand the workings of city maintenance, waste and water treatment, weekly lab test, and general information of town management. In Winthrop, work with Rich Karro and John Haase. In Twisp, work with Gary McConnell.

Graphics: Wolf Prints & Graphics—Students will participate in all aspects of the custom textile design and screen printing business. This fall you will design the T-shirts to be awarded at the Honor Night for all volunteer instructors. Be ready to sign up for spring trimester and print the T-shirts. You will work with Janet Lindsey and Paula Christen.

Trail Building: Help create a horse or hiking trail to bring tourism into the Methow Valley. This trail is being built in Mazama by Goat Wall. You will be putting up signs, building a trail, stacking brush, and having a great time in the out-of-doors. There is potential for summer employment. Get a group of friends together and have a great time. John Hayes will organize.

U.S. Forest Service Classes:

Basic Fire Training—Basic fire training will give you a "Red Card" which will qualify you to work on a private pumper truck or at age 18 make you eligible for employment with the U.S. Forest Service and State Fire Crews. Get advanced training to qualify you as a strong candidate for employment with a fire fighting crew. Attendance is mandatory. You will be given an application and instructions on filling it out. Hands-on experience will be required in the spring on MVCR days(May 12 and 13). Getting a job with the Forest Service could give you a lot of overtime, which means $$$$$, and you could also travel anywhere in the United States, including Alaska. Jim Melton will be your coordinator.

Cartographic and Computer Skill Analysis—Learn more about another computer application system. Work with Meg Trebon at Forest Service (Winthrop) identifying winter recreation trails and mapping them on the Geographic Information System (GIS). Pack a lunch or bring $.

Trail Maintenance—Be involved in the beautiful Methow Valley by maintaining forest trails: cut logs, clear drains, tread maintenance and remove brush. Jim Hammer is a great person. Get a crew and get out in the woods. Pack a lunch.

Wildlife Biologist—Learn a little about special habitats, streams, deciduous trees, old growth, deer cover, fawning cover, migration routes, threatened or endangered and sensitive species. Dawn Zebley (Winthrop) and John Jakubowski (Twisp) will instruct. Pack a lunch.

Management of Timber Land—Discuss tree growth, look at insects and diseases that affect forest health, examine the information we get from ground vegetation, and develop a "silvicultural prescription" for the area. Connie Mehemel will instruct. Pack a lunch.

Range—Christine Bauman will show you how the Forest Service manages the land where farmers graze their livestock. Pack a lunch on May 12. On Thursday, May 13, go to the auction in Okanogan. Pack your lunch.

Veterinary Science: Spend time with veterinarians Dan DeWeert or Betsy Devin Smith and see biological sciences in action.

(continued)

Table 8 (continued)

Informational Classes

Firearm Safety, Rifle Range Basics: The course will cover firearm handling, safety, and more advanced marksmanship skills. We will be doing extensive field work and learning/training that will allow the students to become more proficient and safe firearm handlers and marksmen/women. You must have a Hunter Safety Certificate, bring a 22 cal. rifle, 2-4 boxes of .22 cal. ammunition, bring a sack lunch, and wear clothing appropriate for all-day outdoor activities. If you have further questions contact your instructor, Dr. Bob Maves.

First Aid and CPR: This training will certify you with a Basic First Aid Card. Cindy Button of Aero Methow Rescue will coordinate and help teach the class.

History of the Valley: Learn from historians of this valley. Schedule will be:

May 12 from 9:00 to 11:30 at the home of Carolyn Hotchkiss. Ask about Indian artifacts.

May 12 from 1:00 to 3:00 at the home of Barbara Duffy.

May 13 from 9:00 to 11:30 at the home of Marge White. Marge is a journalist, and you may go visit Gwennie Yockey (born and raised here, she's 93).

May 13 from 1:00 to 3:00; Barbara Duffy will give you a tour of the Museum.

Horse Training: Learn horse training from Nancy Paliorutte. Pack a lunch.

Horse Education: Learn from Sheril Cairns about feeding, handling and training, tack, handling equipment, fitting a horse. Go for a horse ride. Pack a lunch.

Law Enforcement: Learn about law enforcement from all agencies in the valley.

Twisp Police—Keith Roe

Winthrop Police—Bob Gaines

County Sheriff's Office—Dave Rodriguez

Defense Attorney—Rolf Borgerson

State Police—Lee Pilkinton

Women in the Police Force, Introduction to the Juvenile Court System—become informed about training required, police academy training, and officers' "war stories." Kristy Walker and Laura Wright will instruct.

How to Invest Money: Save, save, save or spend, spend, spend. Buy and sell a house; purchase insurance for you, your family, your home and find out just how much insurance you need for a Porsche; open a bank account and take out a loan; and get a good lawyer to keep everything legal and make your own will. You will be learning from Sheila Coe, realtor; Terry Karro, lawyer; Rob Mellish, banker; and Mike Bourn, insurance agent.

Modeling: Modeling is a complex occupation. Learn make-up for day and night, hair styles for night and day, body language, clothing styles with accessories, and do a photo session. Your model will be Mercedes Schmekel.

Newspaper: Produce a four-page student newspaper (*The Roar*) of professional quality. Students will learn skills in editing, newspaper layout (PageMaker), graphic design, photography, and other skills necessary in newspaper production. Work with Greg Knott.

(continued)

Table 8 (continued)

The Outdoor Environment: Hillary Lyman and Jeff Hardy have been trained in Environmental Education to help young people of our school to become informed and to enjoy
and respect the environment. Games will be played to use ALL senses to understand
and respect the beautiful Methow Valley. The class will present and explore opposing
viewpoints with the purpose of coming to some consensus. A real look at the local water
issue will be used as an example. All classes will be outdoors.

Physical Appearance: Visit and learn from several licensed beauticians in their salons.
Enjoy demonstrations of manicures, pedicures, and facials. You will visit the Trim Line
(Abbie Miller), Suite 201(Pat Bost), and Dawn's Hair (Dawn Jones). Patsy Rowland, with
assistance from Mary Kay and Sue Sabin, will share the business part of Avon and have
a makeup session.

Pottery: Be an apprentice at Almquists' Old Time Pottery Studio.

Production Design: We will study a broad spectrum of theatre, both American and
international. Primarily, we will roll up our sleeves and get down to dissecting what it
takes to develop your idea and see it through to fruition. Whether you are interested in
backstage work, staging and light design, costuming and makeup, character development, dance, opera, musical theatre or script writing, we'll identify the components of
theatre production. Bring your creative mind to class each week and let's have fun with
theatre. Theresa Miller invites you to attend.

Promoting Small Business: Enjoy John Monica in learning his job of advertising and
promotion, advertising copywriting, graphic design, management and marketing
consulting.

Pilot Ground School: Teachers and pilots Ginny Wagner, Paul Wagner, Cory Lester, and
Bob Hoffman will give you an introduction to flying.

Radio Technician: Work with Jerry Sabin, retired forest service radio technician, on ham
radio operations and basic electronics. If you learn fast you may troubleshoot. If you are
interested, Jerry will share how to get a ham radio license. Jerry works at OK Cascade
maintaining their electronic equipment.

Sign Language: This class, taught by Barbara Irvine, will introduce you to basic signing
using American Sign Language. Finger spelling, counting, and approximately 150 basic
signs will be learned during the 8-week class. Because there will be class participation
and each class will build upon previous classes, it will be essential that the student do
some amount of practice and weekly preparation.

Slide/Tape Program Production: Under the direction of Bill Moody, students will be able
to produce a professional quality lapse dissolve slide tape program with music/narration
accompaniment. This would be good for seniors for graduation. Limited to 3 students.

Test-Taking Skills for SAT and PSAT: Janie Westlund, Kelly Mellish, and Sara
Borgerson will help you improve your score by practicing the skills needed for taking this
type of test, which is required by most colleges. The tests will be given Oct. 24 at Liberty
Bell High School. $17.00 for the book.

(continued)

Table 8 (continued)

Community Service

Bike Rodeo: Prepare for rodeo, put out posters, advertise. This can be a service to the community. Cindy Button is your instructor. Your help will be needed at the bike rodeo in May. Pack a lunch or bring $.

Build Wood Boxes: Phil Ager will instruct you on making boxes for the Winthrop Forest Service. These boxes will be used as pick-up boxes for information tourist tapes of the North Cascade Pass. You will create a design, determine materials needed, order materials, measure and cut the pieces, and assemble each box. This is a good example of a service project for the community.

Flower Arrangement and Decorating: Enjoy getting greens from the forest. Learn flower arrangement. Make bows, vase coverings, and balloon bouquets. You will be decorating the Barn for the recognition night for volunteer instructors. Monica Bernhard will help you develop your artistic talents.

People Helping Skills: Visit the elderly in their home, senior center, nursing home, and the hospital. Doug Lewis will coordinate the class. Others helping with the class will be Chris Breuninger, Gordy Hutchins, John Smith, Warren Law, and Jess Hinze.

Senior Citizens: Be involved with the senior citizens, play cards, visit, help, and just relate to the older people of our valley.

Special Children: Work with Vicki and Ed Welch with their very special child. They will also share the aspect of their Green House and organic farming.

Special Friends Program: Special Friends Program pairs high school students with individual elementary school children who might benefit from special relationships with older student role models. Interested high school students will be interviewed in order to help them further understand the program. David Asia will give you special training.

Storytelling: Learn how to be an effective storyteller. Carol Bickford and Wordworks Storytellers will be your instructors. Your class will meet at the Winthrop Library—the building with the Little Star School. (This class will require about 2 hours of reading children's books a week.)

Teaching Assistant: Work with teachers by helping young children read, do math, draw, and even just be a good friend. There will be a short training class before the full days.

Leisure and Recreational Activities

Art or Painting: Do a project or paint a picture. Class is taught by Debra Featherston.

Art, Painting: You will help paint a geometric mural above the Confluence Gallery. Even if you think you can't draw, this is an easy, fun learning experience. You will be sharing in a service to our community by painting this mural. Sharon Cohen instructs this class in cooperation with the Confluence Gallery.

Backpack Trip: This overnight backpack trip is based on the Outward Bound model. You will hike 5-10 miles round trip. Your instructor is Outward Bound coordinator Rita Kenney. Tammie Ellis will assist.

(continued)

Table 8. (continued)

Cross-Country Ski Team: Regular training sessions at Sun Mountain ski trails. Poles, skis, and boots will be provided. Also learn how to skate ski from some of the nation's best instructors. Don Portman and Brent Alumbaugh will be your coordinators.

Environment Education Day Hike: You will go on two different day hike trips. Plant identification will be emphasized along with field journal-keeping techniques. Rest of the time will be spent exploring environmental literature and writing. Jess Lindauer will be your tour guide. Pack a lunch.

Floral Design: Learn design from Terry Probst, who just opened a small flower shop in Twisp. The class will involve dried flowers.

Flower Arrangements: Have fun picking your own flowers, etc. Dry them and make your own special arrangement for yourself or for gifts. You will be working with Jill Moen, Monica Bernhard, and Audrey Hoskins. $5.00 charge for materials.

Jazz Dance: Enjoy exercise and learn interesting routines in dance from energetic Debra DeKalb.

Leather Carving: Carve a leather belt with your own name, or any other creative leather carving that you would like from joyful Bill White. This is an opportunity to learn a new skill to use all your life and a creative way to make gifts.

Line Dancing: Practice your rhythm and timing by learning a variety of dances with 4 count, cha cha, waltz, and double beat steps. The dances you may learn are Boot Scootin' Boogie, Tennessee Boot Scootin' Boogie, Achy Breaky, Electric Slide, Tush Push, Rambler, Tennessee Twister, and Line Waltz. Twilla McGowan and Frankie Waller will be your teachers.

Mountain Biking: Dick Hammel instructs this class at the Virginian. Wear riding shorts or tight leg pants and layers. Bring a fanny pack with a lunch. You will learn the basics of bike riding coupled with safety. Your bike will have a water bottle holder.

Outdoor Activities: Tammie Ellis will organize your activities. Have a fun time hiking, canoeing, rock climbing, and ?.

Racquetball: Learn the game of racquetball and have a good workout. You must have the correct shoes to play on the court. See if you can beat Cari Featherston.

Ski Instructor and Winter Safety: You will be assigned, on a rotating basis, to learn and assist with ski school and help with various aspects of running the ski slope: assist instructor, assist on rope tow, coordinate an obstacle course, participate in a slalom race and costume hat day, assist loading and unloading of Poma Lifts, and possibly assist with cross-country patrol and lessons. Kathy Sackett is your instructor.

Ski Patrol: Help the Loup Loup Ski Patrol cover the hill and care for the skiers. Chris Stern will be your instructor and train you as well as ski with you for fun. You will also be trained some in First Aid.

Woodworking and Sculpture: Bruce Morrison will show you woodcarving. He asks that you have patience, and want to work with your hands. You will meet at his house. Pack a lunch.

- Provide freshmen with an orientation to the MVCR program.
- Provide time for high school teachers to plan, reorganize, meet, and evaluate.
- Recognize the volunteer instructors with an evening of appreciation.

Students choose from a published list of more than 200 course descriptions. The majority of activities are noncredit and driven by the interests of the community and students. For example, a senior who was interested in cosmetology arranged for a class with a local cosmetologist for six students. Students not only gained firsthand experience, but they learned about training opportunities for the future. Because MVCR is for all students, no stigma is associated with being involved in a vocational program instead of a program for college-bound students.

The MVCR program occurs for 5 weeks in the fall, 6 weeks in the winter, and 2 full days in the spring. The fall and winter activities are scheduled for every Wednesday afternoon, providing 2-3 hours of community-based instruction. The spring activities are more in-depth experiences, such as a U.S. Forest Service course in fire fighting that leads to a firefighter's certificate. Students do not get paid for their involvement in MVCR, although contact with employers often leads to summer or full-time employment, as illustrated by this college-bound student's statement:

> There's a course, Basic Fire. It will get you your Red Cross card, which will enable you to be on the fire team for the Forest Service. And that can really help you when you go away to college, because you can work during the summer.

The greatest challenge facing the district is linking MVCR experiences with academic classes and providing academic credit for these experiences. At this writing, no credit linkages have been developed.

Focus group interviews were held with three groups of students. Each group of 10 reflected a cross section of students, including high-performing college-bound and vocational students, as well as students who were at risk of failure. All students praised MVCR, saying that it gave them responsibility, addressed their interests, and provided real-life, hands-on experiences. For example, a student who said she wanted to be a beautician was able to arrange a placement with a beautician in the community. Another student interested in being a physical therapist was placed with a chiropractor. A senior who participated in all four years of the program summarized the general sentiment of the three student focus groups:

> A lot of things have interested me, but Methow Valley as a Classroom has really helped me narrow down on what I want or decide to do with my career. But still, it's pretty wide open. There's so many things to do. It's really nice that you get to touch each area, just a little. It also helps you decide what you don't want to do later on.

When asked about their classroom experiences, however, student responses were less positive. They felt their courses were too textbook and lecture driven, with few opportunities for hands-on learning. Moreover, they felt teachers often failed to consider student interests in classroom activities, thus missing opportunities to develop student ownership and motivation:

> It would be nice if you could talk with your teachers, but usually we don't get a chance because they've got their own things planned. And we can't have our opportunities to do our own thing that will relate to the class because they've already got something planned out.

Other work-based experiences. In addition to MVCR, the district offers numerous other workplace opportunities: Diversified Occupations, Community Resource Training, and employment training for students who qualify based on financial need (through the Job Training and Partnership Act [JTPA]), or who have a disability (through the Department of Social and Health Services/Department of Vocational Rehabilitation). Programs other than the latter two are open to all students at the junior and senior level. Community Resource Training is also available for special-needs students. Students can participate, within school hours, for up to 80 minutes; participation beyond this must be done on the student's own time. Interestingly, according to high school English teacher Claudia Gordon, Community Resource Training has become a vehicle for networking students and adults who have similar interests. For example, a high school student interested in paleontology was placed with a forest service person who had expertise in paleontology. These sorts of arrangements contribute to an equalization of status, with academically oriented kids participating in a vocational track.

The special education teacher, the Diversified Occupations/Community Resource Training program coordinator, and the MVCR coordinator collaborate closely. Diversified Occupations and JTPA programs, however, offer wage-paying jobs with the rate of pay established by the employer (no student has received below a minimum wage).

Community Resource Training students have specific plans and objectives they must meet, and they receive credit for their workplace experiences. Employers establish the criteria for passing Diversified Occupation placements and receiving course credit.

Getting the Word Out

The success of the school-to-work program, especially the MVCR component, rests with the extensive promotion it receives both formally and informally. Formally, the school-to-work program is built into the school curriculum as specified in the graduation plan and through the scheduled MVCR activities. Freshmen receive an extensive orientation to the program. A class period, Advocacy, has been built into the schedule to provide time for communicating about events and to counsel students, and students and staff complete many evaluations and accountability forms. Students plan and host a community-wide appreciation night for volunteers. Informally, a network of both students and adults spreads the good word about the program.

The Community Resource Training program coordinator ensures placement and involvement of special-needs students. The structure and nature of the MVCR program provides an ideal environment for promoting and addressing student interests and needs. In fact, MVCR appears to work best with those students who have trouble succeeding in a traditional academic setting. Focus group interviews suggest that MVCR may be a key reason why some students have stayed in school. Several students pointed out that if it were not for MVCR, they would not be in school.

Curriculum. The basic core curriculum has expanded to include STW activities, most notably MVCR. But other activities, presented below, also address postsecondary life skills. At the freshman level, Community Resource Training is often used to help place special-needs students, although at years 3 and 4, regular students may opt for Community Resource Training experiences.

Year 1:

Freshman orientation to high school, Career Pathways, and MVCR

Participation, on a limited basis, in MVCR

Basic core academics

Personal Choices

Information processing

Reading for lifetime skills

Community Resource Training for special-needs students only

Electives: music, art, and trades

Year 2:

Full participation in MVCR

Computer technology

Basic core academics

Reading for lifetime skills

Community Resource Training for special needs students only

Electives: music, art, and trades

Year 3:

MVCR

Basic core academics

Reading for lifetime skills

Community Resource Training

Diversified Occupations

Electives: music, art, and trades

Year 4:

MVCR

Basic core academics

Reading for lifetime skills

Community Resource Training

Independent living or Diversified Occupations

Electives: music, art, and trades

All community-based workplace experiences follow a planned curriculum. Community volunteer instructors develop a written set of expectations for their courses and share them with each student. Some plans are elaborate and detailed, as found in the Forest Service's fire fighting certificate program. However, most plans are less elaborate because instructors are experts in their fields, relying less on written plans and more on learning by doing.

For example, a software engineer offered a course in programming that was embedded in an existing programming job. Students were shown commands and given an opportunity to practice. "Students quickly familiarized themselves with the commands I showed them, and even started using others that they noticed in the manual," noted the instructor. "By the end of the class, each student had written a program for editing data." Through this experience, students got a taste of what it is like to work in an office as a programmer.

The MVCR program incorporates a coordinator who works with students, the school counselor, teaching staff, and parents to ensure the best placement in the community, including the creation of new community-based activities to meet emerging student needs. In addition, an advocacy period has been built into the block schedule. This time is used for boosting reading skills and addressing MVCR curriculum needs within the existing academic schedule. In many ways, it also serves as a homeroom for teachers to counsel students.

Guidance and career development. All students complete a graduation plan that lays out their program of studies for the 4 years and includes vocational options provided within the school's academic program. However, it is MVCR that appears to provide students with the broadest exposure to vocational experiences addressing their personal career and life interests. As freshmen, students participate in an intensive orientation to MVCR that includes team-building activities and participation with older students.

With more than 200 community-based options to choose from, students are generally able to match their interests with the appropriate field experiences. Where their interests differ from available activities, every effort is made to develop an option to address their interests. Based on interviews with students, the team found that MVCR works very well in meeting their interests and helping them discover possible career options for the future. Only about 5 percent of high school students choose to take study hall instead of attending the MVCR advocacy period. Diversified Occupations, Community Resource Training, and two courses–Personal Choices and Independent Living–also provide opportunities for career exploration and development.

The school counselor works closely with the MVCR coordinator to ensure that student needs and interests are addressed. This is accomplished through first-hand knowledge; interviewing students, parents, and teachers; and reviewing data from MVCR evaluation documents. The coordinator for Diversified Occupations and Community Resource Training works closely with the school counselor and the MVCR coordinator in addressing the needs of individual students. There has always been an effort to coordinate the diverse opportunities provided through MVCR, Diversified Occupations, Community Resource Training, and counseling services.

During MVCR, students receive vocational and academic guidance through the mentor relationships established with community volunteer instructors. Upon completing a MVCR course, students receive a written evaluation by the instructor that addresses workplace skills such as punctuality, enthusiasm, and politeness. This practice has been in place since the program began in 1991.

Job placement services. Formal job placement processes do not appear to be needed, as the opportunities created by MVCR provide a steady labor pool for employers. In fact, nearly every student interviewed had summer employment because of MVCR. For example, students who become certified as firefighters through the Forest Service's fire fighting class have a head start on employment in the valley. A new source of employment opportunities opened up last year with the development of a resort destination area at Early Winters. Every student who was placed there during MVCR obtained summer employment. Potential employers have the opportunity to try out employees before hiring. In short, MVCR and the way it is structured is its own job placement service.

Staff development. In 1991, STW was envisioned as an integrated element of the total school program. Twenty-First Century and School-to-Work grant monies have been used to realize that vision through extensive staff development opportunities. Although in the intervening 6 years this vision has been maintained, there have been many changes that have slowed progress. As discussed previously, the district entered into a major building program, a new high school principal was hired, and funding opportunities diminished significantly. Moreover, the state legislated new learning guidelines, especially in the area of assessment. All of these demands curtailed staff development opportunities.

Between 1991 and 1995, grant monies supported numerous opportunities that allowed teachers to plan and develop materials together. During this time period, all staff members participated in a collaboratively planned staff development program that occurred during MVCR time. Taking all this time together, staff had an average of 7 days a year to collaborate. Moreover, there was money for extended contracts for summer work. But when the district consolidated all of its schools, many high school teachers found they were also needed to teach middle school classes. As a result, there is no time during the school day when all teachers can collaborate and plan together. Moreover, grant money that had been available for funding summer teacher institutes is less prevalent. For the 1995-96 school year, the district was able to support training opportunities for only 10 teachers.

Conclusion

The MVCR program has been sustained for more than 6 years and continues to be well managed and supervised, winning unanimous support from parents, students, teachers, and every other group. It has received national attention and has been documented by the National Education Association. The program might be transferable to other rural communities similar to the Methow Valley, but care must be taken to ensure broad-based support of all constituent groups. Moreover, the particular mix of people in the valley and school and their commitment to the community and natural environment of the Methow Valley contribute to the success of the program.

Interest in MVCR from outside the district has been high. School staff members have made presentations about the program to state, regional, and national conferences. They have been featured in journals and newsletters, and on national television. Because of the many inquiries and visitors received over the 6 years of implementation, an implementation guide has been developed by the program coordinator and her husband. They have conducted workshops as far away as Alaska.

An overall evaluation of the program reveals many strengths and some concerns:

Program strengths are that Methow Valley as a Classroom

- builds a strong work ethic, student esteem, and confidence;
- develops real-world job skills and student responsibility;
- fills needs in the community, creates community involvement, and strengthens intergenerational relations;
- connects students to the real world and builds awareness of community strength;
- exposes students to diverse career and recreational opportunities, and provides choices that address their personal interests and career experiences;
- develops potential employment;
- provides students with mentors and supportive relations with adults other than teachers and parents; and
- builds both student and community ownership of education.

Program concerns include

- risk factors such as liability and insurance;
- the challenge of helping adults, including teachers, change the way they think about students and learning;
- pressures on time and resources;

- scheduling and transportation difficulties due to lack of direct involvement of middle school programs;
- lack of a meaningful voice for students in the academic program; and
- school-to-work experiences not linked to the academic program.

The Methow Valley School District's school-to-work program provides an excellent example of a school district building on local assets–the people and resources of the Methow Valley. Methow Valley as a Classroom has provided most students opportunities to explore career and recreational interests. Moreover, it has provided local residents the opportunity to work with youth. According to one volunteer instructor who teaches a course on aviation with her husband,

> I think participation in MVCR shows kids that adults in the community are concerned about their welfare. They know that these adults care for them and are keeping an eye on them, both good and bad. We see what these young kids are doing. I think it's good for me to get acquainted with the young people.

Another key factor for program success centers on the role of the coordinator and the structure of the program. Goals and objectives were jointly developed by the community and the teaching staff. Four strands (career and job skills, information, community service, and leisure and recreation) provide a wide range of choices for students. The coordinator understands the community and the needs of students, staff, and community instructors.

Evaluation also helps ensure program growth and effectiveness. Instructors develop lesson plans and evaluate each student. Data helps the coordinator and the school counselor to monitor student involvement and behavior. Students also evaluate community instructors.

MVCR has built-in incentives for everyone involved. Local people have a chance to share what they know and local organizations have an opportunity to meet potential employees. Students gain new insights into their community as well as authentic career exploration experiences that often lead to employment. For teachers, MVCR expands school curriculum beyond what is possible within the walls of the school. It has also created planning time so teachers can work together on instructional improvement.

MVCR has been integrated into existing school-to-work efforts and the academic program. Block schedules have been developed so school-to-work experiences could occur more easily within the school day. Lastly, although MVCR grew from an initial state grant, the program has been institutionalized through changes in school policy and general fund budget support.

CHAPTER 5

Policy Implications for Planning and Development in Rural Settings

Rethinking the Role of the School

Many rural advocates feel a promising direction for community revitalization and survival lies in building and sustaining strong linkages between the community and the school (Hobbs, 1991; Miller, 1993c; Monk & Haller, 1986; Nachtigal, Haas, Parker, & Brown, l989; Spears, Combs, & Bailey, 1990). Rural communities may have a head start in developing these linkages because schools traditionally have played a central role in the life of the communities. Besides providing for basic education, they often have served as a cultural center in the community where athletics, drama, music, and other social activities play a vital part in community life and identity (Stern, Stone III, Hopkins, McMillion, & Crain, 1994; Versteeg, 1993; Spears, Combs, & Bailey, 1990).

However, building partnerships between the school and the community and providing community-based learning opportunities for students remains a challenge. Such efforts are not generally viewed as traditional elements of schooling. The schools examined in this report have begun meeting these challenges by building strong linkages with their communities and meeting the school-to-work needs of youth.

Students benefit from community involvement in multiple ways. They have the opportunity to learn valuable workplace competencies, test out their vocational and recreational interests, and develop meaningful relationships with the adults in their community. Most students also discover summer and part-time employment through the positive relationships they establish with local businesses and organizations. Moreover, the community benefits in multiple ways as well:

- local businesses have increased access to employees who are interested in their line of work;

- adults teach and give back expertise to their communities by mentoring students; and

- local development and other groups receive valuable help from students who participate in completing projects.

Broadus, Saco, and the Methow Valley represent rural communities that are nurturing conditions of trust, mutual assistance, and information sharing, and are thereby increasing the viability and resilience of their communities in meeting the challenges they face now and in the future. By creating opportunities to work alongside adults on important local needs, youth from these communities gain an increased appreciation for where they live and develop skills they will need as tomorrow's leaders and active citizens.

Teachers, administrators, and school boards cooperated to remove barriers and otherwise facilitate the creation of community-based learning opportunities. Changes in their respective communities occurred because they worked together and because adults recognized the value of youth for the future of their communities.

Three Approaches to Building Community-School Linkages

Miller (1993c) identified three overlapping approaches that build strong linkages between schools and communities. Each approach succeeds by crossing boundaries that have traditionally cut off access to the community as a place of learning.

The first approach views the school as a community center, serving as both a resource for lifelong learning and as a vehicle for the delivery of a wide range of services (Everson, 1994). School resources such as buildings, technology, and a well-educated staff can provide a wealth of educational and retraining opportunities for the community. The community school movement of the 1970s, which offered educational opportunities ranging from day care to adult literacy, represented an early manifestation of this approach (Minzey & LeTarte, 1972). In recent years, the idea of school-as-community-center has resurfaced in the concept of integrated family services, where the school serves as a linking agent for the social service needs of rural youth and families (Stoops & Hull, 1993). Services may include health screening, day care, dental treatment, and a host of other health and human services. In Saco, Montana, the school district has been funded for a fiber-optic network linking three remote communities. The network will provide training for health professionals and fire department personnel. Moreover, it will promote resource sharing by linking schools and communities (Miller, 1995).

A second approach uses the community as curriculum. In this model, students generate information for community development by assessing needs, studying and monitoring environmental and land-use patterns, and documenting local history through interviews and photo essays. Nachtigal has written extensively in this area (Nachtigal, Haas, Parker, & Brown, 1989). He notes that community learning helps students value their community. Nationally, the Foxfire network is the most comprehensive approach to community-as-curriculum. Foxfire provides teacher development and a teacher support network (Smith, 1991). It also engages students in learning about their community through direct encounters with its history. In Broadus, Montana, students learned to interview residents and locate and analyze historical documents in order to reconstruct and preserve the historical context of their community for future generations.

School-based enterprise represents a third approach. School-based enterprise places a major emphasis on developing entrepreneurial skills whereby students identify community needs and establish businesses to address those needs. Sher and DeLargy have turned this concept into a comprehensive curriculum program for rural schools called REAL (Rural Entrepreneurship through Action Learning). With the help of REAL, students have set up businesses such as a shoe repair shop, a delicatessen, and day-care centers, providing both employment and a service not previously available (Stern, Stone, Hopkins, McMillion, & Crain, 1994). Like Foxfire, it is a comprehensive program of curriculum, training, and a support network.

These three interrelated approaches provide ways to think about how schools and communities can work together for their mutual benefit. It is within this mutually beneficial setting that rural communities can offer school-to-work experiences where, under normal school conditions, youth might not otherwise be given such opportunities.

These community-based learning experiences provide leadership development, a renewed sense of civic responsibility, and a revitalized sense of community. However, these approaches also reflect a departure from the traditional ways educators and communities have viewed curriculum. Schools and communities that wish to move in these new directions will need new school policies to remove the barriers blocking their efforts.

Strategies for Change

Many of the most innovative community leaders are rediscovering that youth can be essential contributors to the well-being and vitality of the community. Projects that connect young people productively with other youth and adults are now seen to be the foundations upon which healthy communities can be built. But for this task to be accomplished, youth must no longer be relegated to the margins of community life. (Kretzmann & McKnight, 1993, p. 29)

In 1994, NWREL conducted an invitational symposium on community-based learning experiences for youth in rural communities. Twenty-eight youth and adults representing successful community-based initiatives from the Northwest, Georgia, South Dakota, and Colorado participated in the symposium. Six areas of expertise were discussed and shared: (1) broad-based community involvement, (2) community-based curriculum, (3) community development, (4) service learning, (5) school-to-work, and (6) school-based enterprise. Participants worked in small groups to consider two questions:

1. What has contributed to the success of your community-based project(s)?

2. What recommendations do you have for other people considering community-based learning (e.g., community development, service learning, Foxfire, REAL)?

Table 9 presents a summary of participant responses. Attributes and their descriptions have been ranked by level of importance. The attributes represent a set of tightly interrelated and interdependent elements, not a set of independent variables. Nearly every program described by participants included these elements, but with variations in emphasis.

The symposium led to several insights into how communities and schools can work together for community-based learning. First, consultants or technical assistance providers from outside the community work most effectively in helping implement programs such as those described in this book when they operate as catalysts for change rather

Table 9. The Ten Most Frequently Mentioned Attributes Leading to Successful Community-Based Learning for Students

Rank	Attribute	Description
1	Involve and empower students in all aspects of program or project	Students are viewed as important, contributing members of the community. Class time is scheduled so student involvement becomes part of the regular academic day. The community is made continuously aware of student contributions and the skills achieved by their involvement. Students of all ages are involved.
2	Develop broad-based support for the change	Involve local residents in every step of change: project design, implementation, evaluation, and revisions. This means including local experts, "nay sayers/opposition," students, teachers, parents, economic development groups, political affiliations, various age groups, respected and effective leaders, administrators, locals with historical roots, and advocates. The whole community needs to be informed and a support base developed.
3	Identify resources	Identify resources that will move the project forward. Begin with the strengths that exist locally: students, grant writers, technology, individuals with interest and motivation, those who have access to information. Identify needed resources: funding/grants and consultants/outside expertise.
4	Adopt a common vision	Early in the process, adopt a clear vision of where the project is going, especially one that provides common ground across the community. It is especially important that the school and community have a shared vision. There also should be an ongoing assessment of the vision's appropriateness, with adjustments being made as necessary.
5	Have a structured process	There needs to be a clearly definable management structure to organize the community development process. Activities cannot be random. There must be a process to build vision, identify strengths and needs, set goals, create time to share, build commitment, learn group processes that provide for equitable sharing of ideas from across the community, and adequately plan. Consider hiring a project coordinator.
6	Emphasize group process and team effort	Cooperation and consensus are necessary. They require creating a safe, positive meeting environment characterized by good group process. This means creating an open, honest dialogue among community members through training, team building, conflict resolution, sharing models, and visiting others who are successful.

(continued)

Table 9 (continued)

Rank	Attribute	Description
7	Develop and maintain community (students, residents, and educators) awareness of strengths, needs, and projects	Develop a realistic picture of the conditions existing in the community that require action. Help residents become aware of local resources and student consultations. Help students develop an understanding of the strengths and values of the community.
8	Identify and develop local leadership	Identify people in the community and school who have energy, push, and community credibility. They need to be able to communicate the shared vision. Form a leadership team to help structure activities.
9	Celebrate accomplishments on an ongoing basis	Document and publicize successes in a planned way. Make this part of evaluation and assessment activities. Everyone should feel rewarded by their participation, and efforts should lead to positive community change.
10	Create a productive, safe climate for change	Build and sustain positive relationships. Meetings should take place in a safe, positive environment where all ideas are honored, accepted, and processed. People need to feel it is okay to take risks. There needs to be motivation to change.

than prescribing a course of action. Second, developing grass-roots support among the diverse constituent groups provides a strong foundation upon which to build lasting community-based learning experiences. And finally, all too often, a major gulf exists between schools and their communities. In such cases, recognizing and crossing that gulf must be a major focus of effort and usually requires several actions:

- Link curriculum requirements to community development activities.

- Support teachers with time and resources to develop connecting activities.

- Recognize teachers who incorporate community-based elements into their classrooms, even if they don't directly participate in community activities.

- Demonstrate results early in the process. Early results may include small wins—such as the capacity to work in small groups, write grants, and assume leadership—as well as product outcomes such as a new park, a newsletter, or a tutoring program.

- Demonstrate the belief that both schools and communities see their youth as valued, active members.

- Recognize that public and private institutions, schools, municipalities, and businesses all function under different policies that must be taken into consideration.

All of these policies can have an impact on local efforts to improve schools for youth. School policies are the next focus of this discussion.

The Importance of Policy in Creating and Sustaining
Community-School Linkages

Policy, simply defined, is permission or resources. As permission, there are three types:

- **may**–a policy that makes something possible or enables action, such as a school board resolution to participate in a program of community service;

- **may not**–a policy that repeals permission or restricts action, such as a school board directive that prohibits students from leaving the campus during school hours; and

- **must**–a policy that requires action, such as a state policy requiring all students to be covered by insurance when they are involved in school-sponsored activities. (Murphy, 1995, p. 3)

Many policies also contain resources such as personnel, insurance, facilities, or other necessities for implementing or operating a program (for example, a board resolution allowing an empty classroom to be used as a community resource room). Favorable policies increase the likelihood that a program will be implemented and sustained over time. Such policy also lends credibility to an effort. Murphy (1995) suggests policy serves five essential purposes:

1. helping institutionalize programs and thus improve the likelihood of sustainability;

2. providing resources that can help programs develop and expand;

3. granting permission to act, thus making it easier for programs to develop and grow;

4. providing a legal basis upon which to generate resource support from the private sector; and

5. lending credibility and legitimacy to programs. (p. 4)

Several examples will help to illustrate how these five policy aims can contribute to the success and survival of community-based education projects. In Broadus, Montana, the school board passed a resolution to participate in the project. In addition, other sponsoring organizations such as the economic development council and the mayor were asked to send a letter of support and participation. Taken together, these letters granted permission and support for the communities and schools to participate. Moreover, these endorsements provided a basis upon which to request additional funding from other agencies, businesses, and organizations.

In the Methow Valley School District, school officials wrote a grant proposal that provided state funding for the Methow Valley as a Classroom program. The school board passed a resolution endorsing the grant. After 3 years of implementation, the program had developed broad-based support and acceptance. However, funding prematurely ended because of a legislative cutback. In response, the school board incorporated the cost of running the program into the general fund budget, thus putting the program on a more solid footing. Because of the community's overwhelming support of the program, the school board granted permission and resources for continued operation.

In Saco, Montana, students seeking support for creating a community recreation center worked closely with the superintendent and principal. Students formed parent and student advisory boards to help guide program development that included design and policy components. When students wrote their Serve America grant proposals, they secured permission from their advisory boards and the board of education. As a result, board resolutions supporting the student project of a recreation center provided credibility and visibility to the project.

These illustrations demonstrate the pivotal place policy plays in program development and survival. Moreover, they reveal that program design, implementation, and survival must become a group or collaborative endeavor if it is to be sustained.

Strategies for Developing Effective Policy Support

Murphy (1995, pp. 1-10) describes seven general strategies that have been effective in the development and implementation of community service-learning projects across the country. Although these tactics grew primarily from state-level policy development, they provide a useful framework for thinking about policy creation at the building and school district levels. What follows is a brief description of each strategy and an illustration of its use drawn from rural community-based program development efforts.

Capitalize on the effectiveness of youth as advocates and policy makers. Allow students and those affected by the program to speak for themselves, describing why they need a policy supporting community-based learning.

Example: In Broadus, Montana, students serving on a community development task force for building linkages between local businesses and the school developed a plan for career shadowing. Students presented their plans and illustrated how career shadowing would benefit both students and local businesses. As a result, board policy was written that granted permission for the project, including allocation of resources such as time, insurance, and travel.

Build coalitions. A single individual may have some influence on program and policy development, but single individuals cannot do it alone. A cross section of individuals, groups, and organizations can build a power base that demonstrates to policymakers the value of a project.

Example: In Tonasket, Washington, a community council had been created in order to implement a community development partnership between the community and the school district. Advocates formed a coalition that included the Tonasket Economic Development Committee, the city mayor, the school board, and a broad base of individuals. The coalition was able to leverage resources from the state's economic development department for hiring a project coordinator.

Be patient and persistent. Change requires persistent, long-term commitment. Murphy notes that in Minnesota, "It took five years from the first serious discussion on developing a state youth service policy to the passage of comprehensive youth service legislation" (p. 7).

Example: In 1991, students in Saco, Montana, informally began discussing the idea of having a place for students and the community to go for recreation. In 1995, a recreation center designed and developed by students opened on the community's main street.

Educate public officials. The success of a policy is dependent on individuals who have adequate knowledge and understanding of the issues relating to the policy. Helping those individuals who can influence policy decisions is key. Invite officials to spend time with projects, students, teachers, and community advocates who have knowledge and experience. Seeing and hearing is often more influential than reading.

Example: In Cottonwood, Idaho, a community-school development partnership has been implemented. A recreation task force presented its ideas for a summer youth and family recreation program to a cross section of the community, including the school superintendent and school board representatives. The task force proposal recommended the program be held at the local elementary school and be staffed by volunteers. Support for the summer recreation program was unanimous and the school board adopted policies that made available school facilities and materials.

Use the budgeting process as a policy tool. The budget process provides an excellent opportunity for establishing priorities. These priorities drive the policy agenda for the organization and/or the community. Linking existing priorities to new efforts can create more return on the dollar.

Example: In the Methow Valley, money was reallocated to support the Methow Valley as a Classroom program when the existing state grant ended. By demonstrating to the school board and the budgeting committee that the program provided career and job exploration opportunities not available elsewhere, advocates were able to secure funds to continue the program.

Cover all bases. Ensure that all constituent groups who can influence the policy effort be involved and/or understand and support the effort (or at least are not against it). Sometimes, not being included can lead to opposition. Key constituents to consider are the teachers' association, administrators, parent and community groups, state agencies, and influential individuals.

Example: When the task force for community-school relations in Tonasket wanted to buy a local building and turn it into a community center where youth, especially those who had dropped out or were at risk of dropping out, could go, they sought support from their local government through the mayor. The task force formed a board of directors, wrote bylaws, and obtained nonprofit status. The center is now in its 3rd year of operation.

Do your homework. Solid information and data are more effective than passionate appeals alone. Policymakers would rather hear, in concrete and demonstrable terms, why your program should be granted policy status. However, data need not always be in terms of statistics or numbers. Data can be in more qualitative formats, such as interviews and documents, that show how a program has affected or may affect students and the community.

> Example: In Broadus, Montana, the community council held a conference on the impact of external trends on rural communities in Montana. State tourism and transportation specialists, a rural demographer, environmental groups, coal development advocates, and a school-to-work specialist participated in the conference. More than 80 community residents attended the conference, which was followed the next day by a heavily attended community meeting. Meeting participants created a community-school development vision to guide the work of their community-school partnership.

Conclusion

Rural schools, working in partnership with local leaders and residents, can have a positive impact on community viability. The most successful efforts, such as those found in rural communities like Broadus, Montana, or the Methow Valley in Washington, have sustained their programs far beyond the formative stages by ensuring provisions in school district policy that grant them permission and resources to exist.

The test of success for such programs is determining whether a new and empowering partnership between the community and school has been created that can meaningfully impact the lives of rural youth and adults over an extended period of time. To bring this about, policymakers must recognize that partnerships that engage students in community-based learning require changes in the way schools prepare rural youth for the future. Programs like Foxfire and REAL may provide a beginning curriculum framework. They can help teachers and students see the potential value of community-based learning and pave the way for greater involvement in school-to-work activities.

Community needs and school needs are interrelated. This intersection of needs can create opportunities for the community and the school to work together to benefit students. In rural areas, the school is often the single largest employer and the biggest consumer in the community. The community may also depend on the school for a variety of cultural and recreational opportunities such as athletics, theater, music, and other activities. On the other hand, the school depends on local citizens in order to operate because, unlike urban areas, which often have a large commercial tax base, rural communities must depend on local taxpayers. Thus, any movement toward building and maintaining links between schools and the communities within which they operate can only work to the benefit of everyone involved.

APPENDIX A

Using SCANS as an Interpretive Framework

The Secretary's Commission on Achieving Necessary Skills (SCANS) provides a conceptual framework for viewing the kinds of competencies and skills students in each case-study community were developing as a result of their involvement in school-to-work programs and activities. Interestingly, in these communities it was observed that many opportunities were provided for developing school-to-work competencies, but were not viewed as such. By using SCANS as a lens for viewing school and community learning experiences, we heighten local awareness of existing and potential school-to-work opportunities. For example, when students in an English class help a local chamber of commerce develop a tourist brochure, they are learning school-to-work competencies such as information acquisition and organization and applying foundation skills such as reading and writing. However, when we fail to recognize valuable school-to-work learning experiences, we miss important opportunities for reinforcing awareness of how learning relates to real life. In Tables 10-12, each key activity has been rated for the degree to which it provides opportunities for students to encounter a SCANS competency or foundation area. Representatives from each community helped complete the ratings. A 3-point rating scale was used: H means the activity provided a high level of opportunity; M indicates a medium level; L means a low level; and V indicates a lot of variation.

Table 10 provides an overview of the key activities occurring in the Broadus community. "CDP process and activities" refers to the community-wide meetings, Community Council training and regularly scheduled meetings, and the homework required between each key event in the Community Development Project (refer to Table 3 for a review of these events). The other activities are self-explanatory and may be reviewed in chapter 2, the case study on Broadus, Montana.

Table 11 presents an overview of the relationship between SCANS workplace competency and foundation areas and a sampling of the opportunities offered at the Saco schools discussed in chapter 3. It should be noted that the case study focused primarily on middle- and high-school-level programs. However, interview data suggest that many of the areas included in Table 10 were being addressed at the lower grades, especially the area of technology use.

Table 12 presents key activities occurring in the Methow Valley School District. Chapter 4 explains the four strands of the Methow Valley program. Because the content for each opportunity varies in duration and quality, it is difficult to be precise in assigning a rating. For example, the U.S. Forest Service offers students certification as fire fighters. However, students must enroll in all the weekly sessions as well as the 2-day session offered in the spring to obtain the required hours. There are numerous courses that follow this pattern. There are also short, exploratory activities such as oil painting and snowboarding that are one-time only events, although students may sign up more than once.

Table 10. The Relationship Between SCANS Competencies and Broadus Activities

Competency Area	School/Community Activities				
	CDP Process and Activities	Task Force Committee Activity	Career Shadowing	Community Development Course	Cross-grade Tutoring
Resources—allocating time, money, materials, space, and staff	H	V	L	H	V
Interpersonal skills—working on teams, teaching others, servicing customers, leading, negotiating, and working well with people from culturally diverse backgrounds	H	H	L	H	H
Information—acquiring and evaluating data, organizing and maintaining files, interpreting and communicating, and using computers to process information	M	V	L	H	H
Systems—understanding social, organizational, and technological systems; monitoring and correcting performance; and designing or improving systems	M	V	L	H	M
Technology—selecting equipment and tools, applying technology to specific tasks, and maintaining and troubleshooting technologies	L	L	L	V	L
Foundation Area					
Basic skills—reading, writing, arithmetic and mathematics, speaking, and listening	V	V	M	V	H
Thinking skills—thinking creatively, making decisions, solving problems, seeing things in the mind's eye, knowing how to learn, and reasoning	H	H	V	H	H
Personal qualities—individual responsibility, self-esteem, sociability, self-management, and integrity	H	H	H	H	H

Degree activities address SCANS areas: H = high   M = medium   L = low   V = varies

Table 11. The Relationship Between SCANS Competencies and Selected Saco Activities

Competency Area	School/Community Activities				
	Freeman's Tech-nology Program	Recreation Center Development	Distance Learning EDUNET	Computer Applications	Information Luncheons
Resources—allocating time, money, materials, space, and staff	H	H	V	V	H
Interpersonal skills—working on teams, teaching others, servicing customers, leading, negotiating, and working well with people from culturally diverse backgrounds	M	H	V	L	M
Information—acquiring and evaluating data, organizing and maintaining files, interpreting and communicating, and using computers to process information	H	H	V	V	L
Systems—understanding social, organizational, and technological systems; monitoring and correcting performance; and designing or improving systems	H	H	V	M	L
Technology—selecting equipment and tools, applying technology to specific tasks, and maintaining and troubleshooting technologies	H	V	H	H	L
Foundation Area					
Basic skills—reading, writing, arithmetic and mathematics, speaking, and listening	H	H	V	V	L
Thinking skills—thinking creatively, making decisions, solving problems, seeing things in the mind's eye, knowing how to learn, and reasoning	H	H	V	V	L
Personal qualities—individual responsibility, self-esteem, sociability, self-management, and integrity	H	H	L	L	H

Degree activities address SCANS areas: H = high   M = medium   L = low   V = varies

Table 12. The Relationship Between SCANS Competencies and Methow Valley Activities				
	School/Community Activities			
Competency Area	MVCR strands: 1) Careers 2) Information 3) Service 4) Recreation	Courses: Personal Choices, Senior Life Skills, and Applied Math	Diverse Occupations/ Career Training	Integrated Technology
Resources—allocating time, money, materials, space, and staff	V	V	V	M
Interpersonal skills—working on teams, teaching others, servicing customers, leading, negotiating, and working well with people from culturally diverse backgrounds	H	M	H	M
Information—acquiring and evaluating data, organizing and maintaining files, interpreting and communicating, and using computers to process information	V	H	M	H
Systems—understanding social, organizational, and technological systems; monitoring and correcting performance; and designing or improving systems	V	M	M	M
Technology—selecting equipment and tools, applying technology to specific tasks, and maintaining and troubleshooting technologies	V	M	V	H
Foundation Area				
Basic skills—reading, writing, arithmetic and mathematics, speaking, and listening	V	V	V	M
Thinking skills—thinking creatively, making decisions, solving problems, seeing things in the mind's eye, knowing how to learn, and reasoning	H	H	H	H
Personal qualities—individual responsibility, self-esteem, sociability, self-management, and integrity	H	H	H	M

Degree activities address SCANS areas: H = high   M = medium   L = low   V = varies

APPENDIX B

Powder River Region Community Development Goals

1. The Powder River Region will be aesthetically attractive and inviting to residents and visitors. (Committee of eight, including two educators)

2. The Powder River Region will have community members of all ages demonstrate a strong sense of community and civic pride after being exposed to their cultural, social, and historical heritage. (Committee of six, including one educator)

3. The Powder River Region will have active and diverse community and youth recreational opportunities that add significantly to the quality of life. (Committee of 18, including 6 educators and 6 students)

4. The Powder River Region will have a continuum of health care and aging services to meet the needs of people in the service area. (Committee of nine)

5. The Powder River Region will be a growing agricultural community with opportunity for young ranchers. (Committee of eight, including one educator)

6. The Powder River Region will benefit from the promotion of tourism. (Committee of nine, including two educators)

7. The Powder River Region will expand and grow through the development of small businesses and resources. (Committee of 13, including one educator)

8. The Powder River Region will have its youth become intricately involved in the business and governmental activities of the community, as well as its history and their heritage. (Committee of nine, including four educators and two students)

9. The Powder River Region will have a shared focus on the priority of the family and the church. (Committee of eight)

APPENDIX C

Methow Valley as a Classroom: Sample Forms

- MVCR choice form
- Instructor evaluation form of students
- Instructor evaluation form for MVCR
- Student class evaluation form
- Freshman class orientation evaluation form

MVCR Forms
Methow Valley as a Classroom

Please make 4 choices. Only choose two [2] (L) classes.
G stands for Group class (4-15 students in these classes).
L stands for Limited (from 1-3 students in these placements).

My 1st choice is:

My 2nd choice is:

My 3rd choice is:

My 4th choice is:

Arranged own placement:

If you have already arranged your own placement please include the name and phone number of your instructor. It must be approved by Volunteer Coordinator.

Can you drive to your placement?   YES   NO

Please read and sign the following contract:

I hereby agree to participate in the Methow Valley as a Classroom program and abide by the following conditions:

1. To maintain proper personal appearance requirements of the placement in which enrolled.

2. To conduct myself in a manner appropriate for the business/workplace as per rules established by the instructor.

3. To abide by any and all rules and regulations of Liberty Bell High School and community placement programs including those not stated here (Ref. school rules).

4. If driving to placements, to have a travel form on file with Volunteer Coordinator.

5. If riding to a placement with another student, to have a travel form on file with Volunteer Coordinator.

6. To let instructor know about absence ahead of time and call Volunteer Coordinator at school or leave a message at the office. (Student is considered skipping if call is not made.)

    Consequences:

    a. Skipping–for 1 hour skipped, minimum 1 hour detention or placed on work crew.

    b. If 4 hrs. missed of 16 hr. class, no credit is given and sign up for MVCR will be last.

7. To fill out an evaluation form at the end of the trimester.

Student Signature:

Date:

Parent Permission

I have read the contract that my daughter/son signed and I understand that she/he will be off campus on (Dates) as a part of the Methow Valley as a Classroom program. The program is under the supervision of community volunteers that have been carefully screened and selected to work with the students. I approve of my daughter's/son's participation in the session named. I understand that this may involve an increased risk due to additional transportation and/or to the activities involved. (Read information about transportation on back.) I will not hold the district responsible for the increased risk.

Parent's Signature: Date:

Evaluation of Student Participation (by Instructor)
Methow Valley as a Classroom

This evaluation will go into the student's permanent record.

Name of Student _____

	Yes	No
Was your student attentive?	___	___
On time?	___	___
Polite?	___	___
Present at every session?	___	___
Absent without excuse?	___	___
Eager to participate?	___	___

Comments:

Instructor's Name: _____

Instructor's Evaluation of Program
Methow Valley as a Classroom Program

Class Taught:

Name of Instructor:

Address:

Phone:

Did you enjoy participating as an instructor?   Yes   No
Comments :

Would you repeat this class or placement opportunity?   Yes   No

Were you adequately informed about the program?   Yes   No

What expenses did you incur? (This helps LBHS with budget needs.)

What suggestions do you have, including ideas for future classes?

NAME

Quarter?   F   W   S

Student's Evaluation of Class
Methow Valley as a Classroom

CLASS OR PLACEMENT

INSTRUCTOR:

Was this class interesting to you?	YES	NO
Did you get along with the instructor?	YES	NO
Would you take another class from him/her?	YES	NO
Would you recommend this class to a friend?	YES	NO

What was the most important thing you learned and/or enjoyed?

What could the instructor have done better? How?

What could Volunteer Coordinator have done to help you with your placement?

What are your career goals, hobbies, and interests?

Give suggestions for new classes and how to improve MVCR:

Name of class desired

Instructor who might teach

Phone number of potential teacher

Additional comments appreciated. Complete on back.

Student (Freshman) Evaluation of Methow Valley as a Classroom

(Comment about and evaluate each of the activities in which you participated.)

Ropes Course, Outdoor Activities, and Involvement in the Community

1. Name your activity and instructor for SEPT. 21

Was this class interesting to you?	YES	NO
Did the instructor do a good job?	YES	NO
Would you take another class from him/her?	YES	NO
Should we offer this class to next year's freshmen?	YES	NO
Was transportation adequate to your placement?	YES	NO

    Comments:

2. Name your activity and instructor for SEPT. 28

Was this class interesting to you?	YES	NO
Did the instructor do a good job?	YES	NO
Would you take another class from him/her?	YES	NO
Should we offer this class to next year's freshmen?	YES	NO
Was transportation adequate to your placement?	YES	NO

    Comments:

3. Name your activity and instructor for OCT. 5

Was this class interesting to you?	YES	NO
Did the instructor do a good job?	YES	NO
Would you take another class from him/her?	YES	NO
Should we offer this class to next year's freshmen?	YES	NO
Was transportation adequate to your placement?	YES	NO

    Comments:

APPENDIX D

Resource Documents

Bailey, Thomas, & Merritt, Donna. (1993). *The school-to-work transition and youth apprenticeship: Lessons from the U.S. experience.* New York: Manpower Demonstration Research Corp.

A monograph of existing U.S. programs that combine schooling with work, including agricultural education, such as the 4-H, cooperative education, tech prep, and career academy programs.

Cairn, Rich Willits, & Kielsmeier, James C. (Eds.). (1991). *Growing hope: A sourcebook on integrating youth service into the school curriculum* (1st ed.). Roseville, MN: National Youth Leadership Council.

K-12 educators, whether they have years of experience in service-based learning or none, will find this sourcebook useful in developing new service learning programs as part of the curriculum or to improve existing service and service learning programs. This book offers background information, comprehensive definitions, rationale, practical aids, sample program materials, and resource contacts for developing and maintaining service learning programs.

Churchill, A., Morales, D., & O'Flanagan, K. (1994). *School-to-work toolkit.* Cambridge: Jobs for the Future.

This toolkit provides actual examples of tools and approaches developed by program planners from across the country. It is designed around four key sections, each considered essential for the development of a school-to-work program: (1) planning and design issues, (2) structuring the learning environment, (3) launching the program, and (4) roles and responsibilities. Within each section is a set of cards that describe important elements and case examples. A reader will find actual examples of such resources as contracts, training plans, marketing materials, curriculum excerpts, and grant writing strategies.

Commission on National and Community Service. (1993). *What you can do for your country.* Washington, DC: Author.

This report characterizes the current state of community service in this country and the scope of the National and Community Service Act, passed in 1990. Focusing primarily on youth service, this report discusses grants and other actions the Commission has taken, offers strategies for making the transition from theory to practice, and provides direction for the future. (ERIC Document Reproduction Service No. ED 354 409)

Fraser, Byrna Shore, & Others. (1994). *Minor laws of major importance: A guide to federal and state child labor laws.* Dubuque, IA: Kendall-Hunt Publishing Company.

Resources for employers, students, parents and educators, listing federal and state-by-state restrictions and requirements for minors, as well as key federal and state office phone numbers.

Goldberger, Susan; Kazis, Richard; & O'Flanagan, Mary. (1994). *Learning through work: Designing and implementing quality worksite learning for high school students. School-to-Work Transition Project.* New York: Manpower Demonstration Research Corporation.

This technical assistance guide provides the how-to-do-it advice that local education and business leaders need as they work together to define and establish school-to-work programs. This guide offers concrete suggestions on recruiting employers, designing high-quality program components, and responding to implementation challenges. The reader will also find samples of actual student work tasks, learning plans, student-employer contracts, and assessment forms. (ERIC Document Reproduction Service No. ED 369 940)

Hoffinger, Alex, & Goldberg, Charles. (1995). *Connecting activities in school-to-career programs: A user's manual.* Boston: Bay State Skills Corporation.

This is a handbook for people involved in the development of school-to-work initiatives in the community. It offers practical suggestions on how to design and implement the connecting activities component of school-to-work programs. The handbook also gives many examples of how people around the country have solved some of the key problems in starting and maintaining local school-to-work pathways.

Jobs for the Future. (1993). *Minority youth and the school-to-work opportunities act.* Boston, MA: Jobs for the Future.

A paper containing questions and answers focused on the provisions contained in the School-to-Work Opportunities Act regarding minority participation, policy positions, and specific issues of concern to minority youth advocates.

Kendall, Jane C., & Associates. (1990). *Combining service and learning. A resource book for community and public service.* (Vols. I-II-III). Raleigh, NC: National Society for Internships and Experiential Education.

This is a three-volume resource book for anyone who wants to start, strengthen, or support a program or course that combines community or public service with learning. Policies, issues, and programs are discussed in these volumes that cover many levels of community and public service with learning, including colleges and universities, K-12 schools, community-based organizations, public agencies at all levels, and youth agencies.

Kleinfeld, Judith S., McDiarmid, Williamson G., & Parrett, William H. (1992). *Inventive teaching. The heart of the small school.* Fairbanks, AK: College of Rural Alaska, University of Alaska.

Teachers in both small and large schools who want to improve the quality of their classrooms and schools will benefit from the imaginative and inventive programs and ideas in this book. The first section discusses how to take advantage of small classrooms and other resources, including the education available in the local community and environment. The next section looks at taking advantage of state and national programs, such as academic enrichment, interdisciplinary, correspondence study, summer, and social programs. Highlighted in the last section are lists of sources for the reader to contact for more information and assistance.

National School Boards Association. (1994). *Learning by doing: How school districts are preparing students for the new American workplace.* Washington, DC: Author.

This publication reviews results of a national survey on how school districts are preparing youth for the new American workplace. Section I discusses changes in the American workplace and how those changes have affected today's jobs. Section II includes brief descriptions of the many ways school districts are working to ensure that students will have both the academic and vocational skills for the future. Section III includes basic information on school districts that participated in the national survey.

National Transition Network. (1994). *Directory of state systems change projects on transition.* Washington, DC: Federal Resource Center.

Contains abstracts of transition programs for students with disabilities. The projects are located in 30 states, and were funded by the U.S. Department of Education, Office of Special Education and Rehabilitative Services. The abstracts include project activities, project staff, and subcontractors.

Office of Educational Research and Improvement. (1994). *School-to-work: What does research say about it?* Washington, DC: U.S. Department of Education.

A compilation of six commissioned research papers on subjects such as vocational education and employment in Germany, industry-based education as a new approach for school-to-work, and a map of federal legislation related to the school-to-work initiative. (ERIC Document Reproduction Service No. ED 371 206)

Pauly, E., Kopp, H., & Haimson, J. (1994). *Home-grown lessons: Innovative programs linking work and high school. School-to-Work Transition Project.* New York: Manpower Demonstration Research Corporation.

This report describes the efforts of pioneering U.S. school districts and employers that have built programs to help students make the transition from school to work. Sixteen school-to-work programs in 15 communities in 12 states have been described, including a detailed analysis of both the policy and implementation issues. (ERIC Document Reproduction Service No. ED 369 939)

Stern, D., Raby, M., & Dayton, C. (1992). *Career academies: Partnerships for reconstructing American high schools.* San Francisco, CA: The Jossey-Bass Education Series.

Explains the design and function of the career academy that focuses on career preparation. Provides step-by-step guidance for setting up an academy and tells how to build effective school-business partnerships.

Watkins, J., & Wilkes, D. (1993). *Sharing success in the southeast: Promising service learning programs.* Palatka, FL: SouthEastern Regional Vision for Education.

Information on over 30 effective service learning programs in southeastern states are highlighted in this document. Each program includes a description of its project and activities, the connection between service activities and the academic curriculum, a description of the students involved and their roles in the project design and implementation, sources of funding, project results, and other information such as a contact person. (ERIC Document Reproduction Service No. ED 366 727)

References

Alger, E. (1994). Find rural school-to-work opportunities. *Career Pathways Report, 1*(17), 6.

Berryman, S. (1993). Learning for the workplace. In Linda Darling-Hammond (Ed.) *Review of Research in Education, V.19* (pp. 343-401). Washington, DC: American Educational Research Association.

Boland, P. (Ed). (1995). *School-to-work: Equitable outcomes.* Equity in Education Series. Newton, MA: Education Development Center, Inc. WEEA Publishing Center.

Brandau, D., & Collins, J. (1992). *Schooling, literature, and work in a rural mountain community.* Albany, New York: National Research Center on Literature, Teaching, and Learning. (ERIC Document Reproduction Service No. ED 352 663)

Delargy, P., Hubel, K., Luther, V., & Wall, M. E. (1992). *Building communities from within: Schools and economic development.* Fergus Falls, MN: Communicating for Agriculture, Inc.

DeYoung, A. J., & Lawrence, B. K. (1995). On Hoosiers, Yankees, and Mountaineers. *Phi Delta Kappan, 77*(2), 104-112.

Everson, C. (1994). Local governments and schools: Sharing support services. *Management Information Service Report, 26*(5). Washington, DC: International City/County Management Association.

General Accounting Office. (1991). *Transition from school to work: Linking education and worksite training. Report to congressional requesters.* (GAO/HRD-91-105). Washington, DC: Author. (ERIC Document Reproduction Service No. ED 335 539)

General Accounting Office. (1993). *Transition from school to work: States are developing new strategies to prepare students for jobs. Report to congressional requesters.* (GAO/HRD-93-139). Washington, DC: U.S. General Accounting Office.

Haas, T., & Lambert, R. (1995). To establish the bonds of common purpose and mutual enjoyment. *Phi Delta Kappan, 77*(2), 136-142.

Harrington-Lueker, D. (1993). Preserving American know-how. *American School Board Journal, 180*(11), 24-29.

Hobbs, D. (1991). *Exemplary rural school programs in support of rural development.* Symposium presentation at the National Conference on Rural Adult Education Initiatives, hosted by Rural Clearinghouse for Lifelong Education and Development, Kansas City, MO.

Kazis, R. (1993). *Improving the transition from school to work in the United States.* Washington, DC: American Youth Policy Forum. (ERIC Document Reproduction Service No. ED 353 454)

Kretzmann, J., & McKnight, J. (1993). *Building communities from inside out: A path toward finding and mobilizing a community's assets.* Chicago: ACTA Publications.

Lewis, T. (1995). Rise and decline of job-specific vocationalism: Response to Judith Little and Susan Threat. *Curriculum Inquiry, 25*(3), 293-306.

Miller, B. A. (1987). Hard times in Mineral Valley: Rural decline, cooperation, and survival in the Stafford School District. *Peabody Journal of Education, 67*(4), 90-117.

Miller, B. A. (1993c). Rural distress and survival: The school and the importance of "community." *Journal of Research in Rural Education, 9*(2), 84-103.

Miller, B. A. (1993b). *Promising rural practices in School-to-work transition: Portrait One, Broadus, Montana.* Portland, OR: Northwest Regional Educational Laboratory.

Miller, B. A. (1993a). *Community/school development partnership (CDP) project evaluation report of first-year pilot sites.* Portland, OR: Northwest Regional Educational Laboratory.

Miller, B. A. (1994). *Promising rural practices in School-to-work transition: Portrait Two, Saco, Montana.* Portland, OR: Northwest Regional Educational Laboratory.

Miller, B. A. (1995). *Service learning in support of rural community development.* Symposium conducted at the National Service Learning Conference, Philadelphia.

Minzey, J. D., & LeTarte, C. E. (1972). Community education: From program to process. Midland, MI: Pendell Publishing Co.

Monk D. H., & Haller, E. J. (1986). Organizational alternatives for small rural schools: Final report to the legislature of the State of New York. Ithaca, NY: Cornell University.

Murphy, N. (1995). *Designing effective state policies for youth service.* Symposium conducted at the National Service Learning Conference, Philadelphia.

Nachtigal, P., Haas, T., Parker, S., & Brown, N. (1989). *What's noteworthy on rural schools and community development.* Aurora, CO: Midcontinent Regional Educational Laboratory. (ERIC Document Reproduction Service No. ED 313 177)

O'Neil, J. (1995). On preparing students for the world of work: A conversation with Willard Daggett. *Educational Leadership, 52*(8), 46-48.

Owens, Tom. (1995). Grand Coulee Dam School District. In *Washington State School-to-work evaluation report.* (Volume II: Case Study

Report). Portland, OR: Northwest Regional Educational Laboratory, p. 63-75.

Seal, K. R., & Harmon, H. L. (1995). Realities of rural school reform. *Phi Delta Kappan, 77*(2), 119-124.

Secretary's Commission on Achieving Necessary Skills. (1991). *What work requires of schools: A SCANS report for America 2000.* Washington, DC: U.S. Department of Labor. (ERIC Document Reproduction Service No. ED 332 054)

Sharratt, G., McClain, C., & Zehm, S. (1993). Vocational education in rural America: An agenda for the 1990s. *Rural Education, 14*(1), 21-26.

Sherman, A. (1992). *Falling by the wayside: Children in rural America.* Washington, DC: Children's Defense Fund. (ERIC Document Reproduction Service No. ED 367 528)

Smith, H. (1991). *Foxfire-affiliated teacher networks.* Paper presented at the Annual Meeting of the American Educational Research Association, Chicago, IL, April 2-6, 1991. (ERIC Document Reproduction Service No. ED 330 685)

Spears, J. D., Combs, L. R., & Bailey, G. (1990). *Accommodating change and diversity: Linking rural schools to communities.* A report of the Ford Western Taskforce. Manhattan, KS: Rural Clearinghouse for Lifelong Education and Development, Kansas State University. (ERIC Document Reproduction Service No. ED 328 392)

Stern, D., Stone III, J., Hopkins, C., McMillion, M., & Crain, R. (1994). *School-based enterprise: Productive learning in American high schools.* The Jossey-Bass Education Series. San Francisco: Jossey-Bass Publishers.

Stern, J. (Ed.). (1994). *The condition of education in rural schools.* Washington, DC: U.S. Department of Education, Office of Educational Research and Improvement.

Stoops, J., & Hull, J. (1993). *Toward integrated family services in rural settings: A summary of research and practice.* Portland, OR: Northwest Regional Educational Laboratory.

Students involved with community planning process. (1992, November 5). *Powder River Examiner,* p. 7.

Versteeg, D. (1993). The rural high school as community resource. *Educational Leadership, 50*(7), 54-55.

Washington Governor's Council on School-to-Work Transition, Seattle. (1995). *Governor's council on school-to-work transition. Final report.* (2nd Edition). Seattle: Author. (ERIC Document Reproduction Service No. ED 396 090)

Index

academic competitions, 41-42

academic education, 3-5; in Methow Valley, 63, 67, 70. *See also* college preparation

administrators, 80; and community-based learning, 30, 72

agriculture, 3, 53; mechanization of, 2, 7

apprenticeships, 1, 5

athletics, 40-41

BPA (Business Professionals of America), 42

Brandau, D., 8

Broadus, 11, 13-31, 72-73, 78-79, 81; Community Development Project, 14-18; SCANS and, 83, 85 (table)

Broadus County High School: community development course, 23-26; cross-grade tutoring, 26-27; demographic characteristics, 11 (table); recreation center, 24-26

budgeting, 80

businesses: links with schools, 5-6, 79

Business Professionals of America (BPA), 42

career counseling, 1-2, 5

career development, 67-69

career exploration, 5, 40, 49, 56, 70, 80

career shadowing, 18, 22, 79, 85 (table)

Carmichael, Gary, 36

CDP (Community/School Development Partnership), 14-21, 29, 83, 85 (table); progress chart, 17-18

civic responsibility, 73

classroom experiences, 64

coalitions, 79

college preparation, 1, 3-4; in Methow Valley, 56, 63. *See also* academic education

Collins, J., 8

Colorado, 74

communication, 31

community: as curriculum, 73; uprooting, 8-9

community appreciation, 56, 73

community-based learning, 30-31, 71-76, 78, 81; in Broadus, 13, 28; in Methow Valley, 54, 56, 63, 66-67

community center: school as, 72-73

community development, 28, 73-74; in Broadus, 13-31, 79; Powder River Region, 88

community development course, 23-26, 85 (table)

community instructors, 55-56, 63, 66, 68; evaluation of, 70

community involvement, 46-47, 56, 69, 71, 74

community needs, 73, 81

Community Resource Training (CRT), 54-55, 64-67

Community/School Development Partnership (CDP), 14-21, 29, 83, 85 (table); progress chart, 17-18

community-school partnerships, 71, 72-74, 77-82; in Broadus, 14-21, 81; in Methow Valley, 54, 56

community service projects, 6; in Methow Valley, 56, 61, 70; in Saco, 38-39

competencies, 5, 31, 50; in Broadus, 13, 18-20, 85 (table); in Saco, 33, 49; SCANS and, 9-10, 83, 85-87 (tables). *See also* skills; workplace competencies

Computer Assisted Vocational Consortium, 40

computer networks, 35

computers, 34, 36; notebook, 35-36, 43

computer software, 35

consortia, 40

context learning, 51

conventions, 41

cooperative education, 1, 5

correspondence courses, 35

costs, 23; of technological innovation, 40

Cottonwood, 80

counselors, 1, 5, 67

course credit, 16, 21, 23-24, 26-27, 56, 65

Crowder, Larry, 41

CRT (Community Resource Training), 54-55, 64-67

curriculum, 81; community as, 73; community-based, 74; community development and, 76; community development course, 23-26; computer networks and, 35; development, 40; integration, 35, 48; interactive, 5; in Methow Valley, 65-67, 70; recreation center as, 43, 46; in rural schools, 20; SCANS and, 9-10

Daggett, Willard, 4

de-industrialization, 2-3

Department of Education, 5

Department of Labor, 5

Department of Social and Health Services, 64

Department of Vocational Rehabilitation, 64

DeYoung, Alan, 7-8

disabilities, 64

distance learning. *See* EDUNET

Diversified Occupations (DO), 54-55, 64-65, 87 (table)

DO (Diversified Occupations), 54-55, 64-65, 87 (table)

economy, 2-3, 6-7; Broadus, 14, 28; Methow Valley, 54; rural, 4, 7; service, 3

education: adult, 40; ambivalence toward, 7; basic skills, ix; career, 5; higher, 8; postsecondary, 1-2, 4-5, 28; role of, ix, 2. *See also* schools

educational practices, 1-4

educational reform, 4, 8

educational system, 3-5

EDUNET, 35, 37, 49, 86 (table)

electronic mail, 35

employability, 19

employers, 2, 5, 8-9, 31, 65, 68; school as, 81

employees, 70, 72; skills, 2, 31

employment, ix-x, 5, 22, 28, 72-73; in Broadus, 14; in Methow Valley, 55, 63, 68-70; summer, 63, 68. *See also* job opportunities

evaluation, 76; of community instructors, 70; of Methow Valley as a Classroom, 65, 69-70, 92-95 (forms); of students, 5, 27, 68, 92 (form)

extracurricular activities, 8, 34, 40-42

family income, ix

FFA (Future Farmers of America), 6

FHA (Future Homemakers of America), 41-42

financial need, 64

Fladland, Stacie, 42, 44, 46

Florida, 6

FOCUS, 40

foundation areas: SCANS, 9-10, 85-87 (tables)

4-H, 6

Foxfire, 73, 81

Freeman, Dwight, 38, 45-48, 50-51

funding, 7, 23, 78; in Methow Valley, 68, 70, 78, 80; sources in Saco, 38-39 (table), 40

Future Homemakers of America (FHA), 41-42

Georgia, 74
Gordon, Claudia, 64
graduation, 1-2; plan, 67
guidance, 67-68. *See also* counselors

Hahn, Karen J., 113
hands-on experience, 48, 64
Harmon, H.L., 7
higher-order thinking skills, 50
home economics, 48-49
Hutterites, 36-37

individualized instruction, 49
information retrieval, 50
infrastructure, 40
International Center for Leadership in Education, 4
internships, 5
isolation, 6, 8, 13, 15, 34
job opportunities, 2-4; in Methow Valley, 56. *See also* employment
job placement service, 68
job requirements, ix
Job Training and Partnership Act (JTPA), 64
JTPA (Job Training and Partnership Act), 64

Kazis, Richard, 2-4
Knudsen, Carl, 34-37, 39-41, 43, 47, 49

labor force, 7
Lawrence, Barbara Kent, 7-8
leadership, 73, 76; in Broadus, 13, 15, 21; CDP and, 15; organizations, 5-6; in Saco, 33-34, 49
learning, 10; environments, 51; lifelong, 39, 55, 72; objectives, 10; school-based, 5; self-directed, 34; service, 1, 9, 74, 78; work-based, 5, 9, 64-65. *See also* community-based learning
learning to learn, 6, 8, 50
leisure and recreational activities: in Methow Valley as a Classroom, 56, 61-62, 70
Liberty Bell High School, 53
libraries: in Saco, 35
logging, 7, 53

manufacturing, ix, 3

mechanization, 2, 7

mentoring, 5, 9, 53, 68-69, 72

Methow Valley, 53-70, 72, 81; SCANS and, 84, 87 (table)

Methow Valley as a Classroom (MVCR), 54-70, 78, 80, 87 (table); courses and activities (table), 57-62; sample forms, 89-95

Methow Valley School District, 54, 78; demographic characteristics, 11 (table)

MetNet (Montana Educational Telecommunications Network), 35

metropolitan influence. *See* urban influence

migration: to urban areas, 4. *See also* out-migration

Miller, B.A., 72, 113

mining, 3, 7, 53

Minnesota, 79

Montana, 13. *See also* Broadus; Saco

Montana Educational Telecommunications Network (MetNet), 35

Murphy, N., 77-79

music festivals, 41

MVCR (Methow Valley as a Classroom), 54-70, 78, 80, 87 (table); courses and activities (table), 57-62; sample forms, 89-95

Nachtigal, P., 73

National Education Association, 69

National Rural Education Association, 35

Northwest Regional Educational Laboratory (NWREL), 14, 74

NWREL (Northwest Regional Educational Laboratory), 14, 74

occupational trades, 55

Oregon, 6

out-migration, 28

pay. *See* wages

physical education, 55

planning, 24, 31, 71-82; short-term (form), 25

policy, 70, 71-82

poverty, ix, 7

Powder River County High School, 16

Powder River Region: community development goals, 88

problem solving, 8, 10; in Broadus, 20-21, 24; in Saco, 34, 38, 42, 48, 50; and technology, 38 promotion, 65

public school system, 3

REAL (Rural Entrepreneurship through Action Learning), 73, 81

real-world opportunities: In Broadus, 13; in Methow Valley, 53; in Saco, 33, 43, 47-49

recreation centers: in Broadus, 24-26; in Saco, 25, 42, 43-47, 78-79, 86 (table)

research, 1-10

resource documents, 96-99

resources, 30-31, 69-70, 75, 81; community, 6, 9, 11, 20, 55; local, 20; management of, 26; occupational, 20; policy and, 77, 79; rural, 20, 34; school, 15, 55, 72; service as, 38; shared, 73; students as, 15, 19-20

rural communities, viii-x, 4, 6-9, 20, 34, 50, 69, 71-74, 78, 81

Rural Education Program, 14

Rural Entrepreneurship through Action Learning (REAL), 73, 81

rural production, 2

rural schools, viii-x, 4, 6-8, 34, 50, 71, 81

Saco, 11, 25-26, 33-51, 72-73; recreation center, 25, 42, 43-47, 78-79, 86; SCANS and, 83, 86 (table); technology in, 34-40, 42-43, 47-48, 83

Saco School District, 33-36; demographic characteristics (table), 11

SCANS (Secretary's Commission on Achieving Necessary Skills), 9-10, 31, 83-84; and Broadus (table), 85; and Methow Valley (table), 87; and Saco (table), 86

scheduling, 26, 30, 65, 70; block, 54, 67, 70

school-based enterprises, 9, 73-74

school boards, 72, 78, 80

school needs, 81

school organizations: participation in (table), 42. *See also* extracurricular activities

schools: as employer, 81; role of, 71-72, 81. *See also* education

School-to-Work (STW), 54-56, 65, 68

school-to-work initiative, 4-6

School-to-Work Opportunities Act of 1994, 1

Science of Olympiad, 41-42

Seal, K.R., 7

Secretary's Commission on Achieving Necessary Skills (SCANS). See SCANS

service sector, 3

skills: academic, 53; employee, 2, 31; job, 3, 5, 56-58, 69-70; postsecondary life, 65; shortage, 2. *See also* competencies; student skills; workplace skills

social services, 73

South Dakota, 74

special-needs students, 64-66

staff development, 39-40, 68

student enrollment: in Broadus, 14

student intern program, 21-22

student involvement, 50-51, 70; in community development, 16, 19, 23-24, 28-30; in recreation center, 46; teachers and, 16, 19, 23; workplace competencies and, 18-20

student motivation: in Broadus, 19; in Methow Valley, 64

student needs, 28, 42-43, 49, 65, 67, 70-71; postsecondary, 55

student-operated businesses, 6

student portfolios, 9

student skills, 4, 9-10, 16, 24, 28-29, 41-42, 44, 50, 72; SCANS and, 83; in technology course, 48

STW (School-to-Work), 54-56, 65, 68

summer: employment, 63, 68; work-based learning, 9

support, 8, 46, 51, 69, 73; adult, 44-45; for community-based learning, 30, 75-76, 78; for cross-grade tutoring, 27

Talents Unlimited, 20

task forces, 21-23, 85 (table)

tax base, 7, 82

teachers, 63-64, 70, 72, 76, 81; in CDP, 16; collaboration, 35, 68; and community-based learning, 30; and community development, 23; Foxfire and, 73; involvement of, 19-20; role of, 51; and student involvement, 16, 18, 23

technology: course, 47-48, 51, 86 (table); in Saco, 34-40, 42-43, 47-48, 83

Technology Students Association (TSA), 41-42

Tech Prep Consortium, 54

tech-prep programs, 1, 55

telecommunications, 34-36, 40

Tennessee, 6

time management, 24, 26

Tonasket, 79-80

training: job, 5; student, 41; teacher, 5, 39

TSA (Technology Students Association), 41-42

tutoring: cross-grade, 18, 26-27, 85 (table)

Twisp, 11, 53

unemployment, ix, 7

unskilled workers, 2

urban areas, 20, 34; migration to, 4

values, 8, 15-16

vocational education, 1, 3-5; Broadus, 20; Methow Valley, 56, 63, 67; Saco, 47-48

volunteerism, 26

volunteers: community, 46, 65; student, 49. *See also* community instructors

wages, 7, 65

Walters, Diana, 9

Washington (state), 6. *See also* Methow Valley; Tonasket

Washington Occupational Information System (WOIS), 54

Wenatchee Valley Community College, 55

Winthrop, 11, 53

Wisconsin, 6

WOIS (Washington Occupational Information System), 54

workforce production sectors, 3

workplace competencies: community development and, 20; community involvement and, 71; SCANS and, 83; student involvement and, 18-20

workplace experiences, ix, 6, 9, 44; hands-on, 5; in Methow Valley, 64-66; paid, 5

workplace skills, 2, 4, 31, 37; in Broadus, 13, 19-20, 22, 27; in Methow Valley, 68; in Saco, 33; SCANS and, 9-10

YMCA, 43

YWCA, 43

About the Authors

Bruce A. Miller received his doctorate in curriculum and instruction at the University of Oregon in 1985. He currently is a senior research associate in the Rural Education Program at Northwest Regional Educational Laboratory in Portland, Oregon. He has written and published extensively on issues relating to rural schools, communities, and the implementation of multiage instruction.

Karen J. Hahn received her B.S. in Sociology (1992) and M.A. in Sociology (1994) from the University of Wyoming. Ms. Hahn formerly worked as a Research Specialist in the Rural Education Program at Northwest Regional Educational Laboratory. She currently is a Research Associate at RMC Research Corporation where she is involved in the evaluation of several school- and community-based education programs and coalitions addressing violence, alcohol, and other drug prevention.